SpringerBriefs in Well-Being and Quality of Life Research

SpringerBriefs in Well-Being and Quality-of-Life Research are concise summaries of cutting-edge research and practical applications across the field of well-being and quality of life research. These compact refereed monographs are under the editorial supervision of an international Advisory Board*. Volumes are 50 to 125 pages (approximately 20,000–70,000 words), with a clear focus. The series covers a range of content from professional to academic such as: snapshots of hot and/or emerging topics, in-depth case studies, and timely reports of state-of-the art analytical techniques. The scope of the series spans the entire field of Well-Being Research and Quality-of-Life Studies, with a view to significantly advance research. The character of the series is international and interdisciplinary and will include research areas such as: health, cross-cultural studies, gender, children, education, work and organizational issues, relationships, job satisfaction, religion, spirituality, ageing from the perspectives of sociology, psychology, philosophy, public health and economics in relation to Well-being and Quality-of-Life research. Volumes in the series may analyze past, present and/or future trends, as well as their determinants and consequences. Both solicited and unsolicited manuscripts are considered for publication in this series. SpringerBriefs in Well-Being and Quality-of-Life Research will be of interest to a wide range of individuals with interest in quality of life studies, including sociologists, psychologists, economists, philosophers, health researchers, as well as practitioners across the social sciences. Briefs will be published as part of Springer's eBook collection, with millions of users worldwide. In addition, Briefs will be available for individual print and electronic purchase. Briefs are characterized by fast, global electronic dissemination, standard publishing contracts, easy-to-use manuscript preparation and formatting guidelines, and expedited production schedules. We aim for publication 8–12 weeks after acceptance.

More information about this series at http://www.springer.com/series/10150

Jef J. J. van den Hout · Orin C. Davis

Team Flow

The psychology of optimal collaboration

Springer

Jef J. J. van den Hout
Flow Concepts
Tilburg, The Netherlands

Orin C. Davis
Quality of Life Laboratory
New York, NY, USA

ISSN 2211-7644 ISSN 2211-7652 (electronic)
SpringerBriefs in Well-Being and Quality of Life Research
ISBN 978-3-030-27870-0 ISBN 978-3-030-27871-7 (eBook)
https://doi.org/10.1007/978-3-030-27871-7

This Springer imprint is published by the registered company Springer Nature Switzerland AG
The registered company address is: Gewerbestrasse 11, 6330 Cham, Switzerland

Foreword by Mihály Csíkszentmihályi

We human beings have an innate need to connect with each other, and all the more so in individualized Western societies. In an era when trust, respects, support, and psychological safety are both highly prized and difficult to achieve, we are lonelier than ever and in desperate need of a means to connect with one another.

At work we suffer from abuses of power, bureaucracy, politics; from incentives for competition, fear, and low morale; and from a host of other ills that keep us from collaborating effectively. Pigeonholed in jobs that do not allow growth and use of skills, people slack in their work and hate what they have to do.

Looking at the future of our planet, we need talented people to help solve these challenges and reinvent the future.

None of these challenges has an easy solution, but in team flow, there is a key that might help. The ideas and research contained in this book show ways that teams can connect with one another, collaborate effectively, and be empowered to give their best performances.

The acronym TEAM that the authors provide: Together Everyone Achieves More, is a truism that provides a guideline for how humankind can evolve. Through optimal experiences, the possibilities of what teams can accomplish are endless.

Claremont, CA, USA Mihály Csíkszentmihályi

Foreword by Mathieu Weggeman

With this book, which is based on years of scientific study, Jef and Orin are providing a tool that teams can use to increase their odds of experiencing flow at work. And it could not have come at a better time. Millions of workers spend 8 hours a day, 5 days a week, and 45 weeks a year for 40 years working in the organizations around us. Take a human lifetime, subtract 25 years for training and another 25 for retirement and you'll see that people spend roughly a third of their lives working in organizations.

In the advanced economies of the Western world, the following attitude has become increasingly uncommon: "Sure boss, you can tell me what to do between 9 and 5, so long as you pay me enough to do what I really want to do between 5 and 9." We are no longer prepared to barter away that enormous chunk of our time on this earth. Increasingly, workers demand meaning from their work, to know the intrinsic reward of losing themselves in their work. They want to feel that they, and the people they work with, are making the most of themselves. Jef and Orin show what organizations can do to foster those kinds of flow experiences. The book helps leaders and professionals create and manage their teams in ways that increase the likelihood and frequency of collective flow experiences while at the same time reducing stress and apathy.

The central element of their theory is the concept of a collective ambition: to strongly desire the same thing together. A collective ambition is hugely valuable for its ability to motivate professionals and increase job satisfaction, productivity, and cooperation. These are all prerequisites for the team flow experience. A jointly created and broadly supported collective ambition is what opens the door to team flow.

Once there is a collective ambition and team flow is happening, all we have to worry about is beauty: the beauty of our workflows and the beauty of the products and services those workflows produce. Having spent years in the thrall of efficiency drives, quality programs, and the need to maximize stakeholder value, it's about time we considered the aesthetics of our organizations, if only because professionals with an appreciation for beauty foster and experience more team flow than their less aesthetically minded coworkers.

What I hope to see is that modern organizations will come to understand that creating positive aesthetic experiences at work, especially team flow, is a critical success factor.

Eindhoven, The Netherlands Mathieu Weggeman

Preface

Any team seeking to innovate needs to interact smoothly. The reality, however, is that some teams function poorly and have a tremendously negative influence on other people's performances and wherewithal to innovate, which adversely affects the organization as a whole. This is often caused by excessive numbers of procedures, policies, schedules, and control measures or, alternatively, because organizations create self-managing teams and then leave the members of those teams to figure everything out for themselves. This increases the odds and incidence of dysfunction, stress, absenteeism, and burnout. In most cases, what teams need to improve their internal cooperation is support from their leaders. This is why there has been a great surge in demand from many organizations for tools and methods to help teams perform autonomously and successfully.

Research has shown that the psychological experience of flow delivers great benefits in many areas of life, including work settings. To date, however, flow in the workplace has typically been studied at the individual level, whereas the kinds of complex tasks performed in professional organizations are often assigned to teams (whose "team flow" experiences are rarely studied). Despite the noted potential for optimal experiences (i.e., flow) to enhance innovation, creativity, productivity, performance, and well-being, there has been little research on how teams, and especially work teams, can harness the benefits of flow.

Creating the prerequisites of flow for workplace teams could allow teams and organizations to reach new heights of synergy by maximizing their potential. To that end, this book presents a series of studies that conceptualize, test, and monitor team flow experiences, then describes the process by which team flow emerges with exemplifying case studies, and finally introduces a road map and set of guidelines for sparking team flow in professional organizations. How wonderful would it be for team members to experience flow together as they collaborate toward a common purpose?

Tilburg, The Netherlands — Jef J. J. van den Hout
New York, USA — Orin C. Davis

Acknowledgements

We would like to thank a few people for writing this book. First of all Mihály Csíkszentmihályi for his lifelong contributions to the field of psychology (and for introducing us to each other in the first place!). With the introduction of the psychological term "flow," he has given a word to what is a very recognizable experience for many people in our world and one that is very valuable to pursue sustainably. He has also inspired the authors of this book with his work to do very dedicated research into the field of flow, from microflow to team flow. Mihály Csíkszentmihályi also took a seat on the promotion committee during the Ph.D. research of both authors, in the role of supervisor and opponent. Both authors are very grateful to him for this.

Jef J. J. van den Hout

Mathieu Weggeman has particularly inspired me with his research and publications on the management of professionals, especially with stories about what can go wrong when people start to lead highly talented professionals. His most popular book is therefore entitled: *Managing Professionals? Don't!* In one of his articles, Weggeman also introduces the term collective flow as an extension of Csíkszentmihályi's flow. In the vision of Weggeman, managers must above all ensure that "their" people can continue to experience flow during the performance of their work. That this ultimately adds something to the larger whole of the organization can in most cases be relied on for the simple reason that professionals, people who are particularly talented in a certain field, naturally prefer to do something good than something bad. I therefore thank Mathieu Weggeman for his contributions to science as in the role of supervisor of the first author in his Ph.D. research on team flow.

Someone who has succeeded in putting this into practice is Jos de Blok, founder of Buurtzorg Nederland. An organization started with four people in 2006 and has since grown into an organization with nearly 15,000 employees working in teams. It is now known from this organization that the professionals there are performing exceptionally well and are enjoying themselves immensely. I would like to thank Jos de Blok for showing me what the organization of Buurtzorg Nederland is all about. What you need to leave behind to make an organization run smoothly and what you can do to facilitate teams in the cooperation with each other and the execution of their work for their clients, in this specific case people that need healthcare at home. In addition, we also thank Jos de Blok for letting me contact the home care teams within the Buurtzorg Netherlands organization and then unravel the flow with the teams. These interviews have produced very nice interview reports that we share a few of them in this book. We especially thank the members of the team "De Beerzen" from Middelbeers for which we report an extensive description of how they maintain a team flow climate in this book.

In addition, we conducted interviews in the field with Han Schaminee, Victor Middelkoop, and Wim Koch, of which we gratefully describe their moments of team flow in this book. From the scientific field, I would like to thank Bob Walrave, Josette Gevers, Jeanne Nakamura, Jan Walburg, Frans Ørsted Andersen, Joan van Aken, and Ruut Veenhoven. All have contributed in one way or another to this book.

Orin C. Davis

I would like to thank my doctoral advisors and mentors, Mihály Csíkszentmihályi and Jeanne Nakamura, who have been a constant source of wisdom, insight, and support, and always pushed me to translate ideas from the theoretical to the practical. My two advisors were always a great team ensuring that I view everything from both a sky-high perspective and a ground-level perspective. Continuing thanks to my mentors Solomon Diamond and Michael Kahana, who have trained and developed my thinking in more ways than I could enumerate. Thank you to my volleyball coach, Melinda Udell, whose insightful coaching has inspired much of my research on teamwork. Much gratitude always to my family, who have offered innumerable amounts of support, cheering, and humor. This book is dedicated in memory of my grandparents, Bertha (ברכה בת זלמן הלוי וגיטל ז"ל) and Simon (שמעון בן ישעיה הכהן והנדא ז"ל) Shoten, who drilled into me over repeated games of Canasta, *"You play with a partner!"*, and in memory of my grandfather, Max (מאיר בן יוסף ושיינדל ז"ל) Davis, who taught me to make sure my dance partners always got to show their best moves. May their memories be for a blessing!

Contents

About the Authors

Jef J. J. van den Hout (1978) is obsessed with the psychology of flow. Thanks to this obsession, he succeeded in finalizing his Ph.D. research on the theoretical concept of team flow in December 2016. Mathieu Weggeman was his promotor, and Mihály Csíkszentmihályi, the originator of flow theory, was his opponent in the promotion committee. Currently, Jef helps members of professional teams to achieve team flow and organizes events on the topic of flow with designers, entrepreneurs, artists, and musicians (see www.flowconcepts.nl). He is also an associate researcher at Eindhoven University of Technology, investigating team collaborations, and a guest lecturer for executive master's degree programs at Aarhus University in Denmark (positive psychology) and the Erasmus University of Rotterdam (EHERO—Erasmus Happiness Economics Research Organization). Jef has previously studied psychology at Tilburg University and architectural design management systems at Eindhoven University of Technology.

Orin C. Davis (1981) earned the first doctorate in positive psychology and is a self-actualization engineer who enables people to do and be their best. His consulting focuses on making workplaces great places to work through effective hiring processes, employee engagement, enhanced creativity and teamwork, and diversity and inclusion; his coaching centers around careers (personal branding, career trajectories, and personal/professional development); and his research is on flow, creativity, hypnosis, and mentoring. In addition to being the principal investigator of the Quality of Life Laboratory, he is a startup advisor who helps early stage companies enhance their value propositions, pitches, culture, and human capital. Orin Davis also serves as a science advisor to Happify and an adjunct professor of business, psychology, entrepreneurship, and creativity. He writes and speaks avidly about human capital, creativity/innovation, and positive psychology.

Chapter 1
An Introduction to Flow Theory

This first chapter introduces the foundations of flow, what it is, and which research already exists regarding this phenomenon. This chapter highlights the importance of flow in everyday life and explains why people can benefit from experiencing flow in their work activities. We then show how flow is beneficial to groups, and especially for teams in the workplace.

1.1 The Flow Experience

Have you ever found yourself so engrossed in an activity that the roof could have fallen in and you wouldn't have noticed? Time and space fall away, and you are "in the zone". Nothing matters but the activity you're doing, and, as hard as this task is, you're making serious progress and you know it. You could do this all day, and when you're done, you feel fantastic. If that sounds familiar, you are one of the many people who has experienced *flow*.

Also known as *optimal experiences*, moments of flow are among the most enjoyable elements of daily life. They often involve peak levels of performance, which not only feels great, but also tends to lead to better outcomes. In flow, we're pushing ourselves, striving for mastery, and reveling in the results. Ironically, we don't love every minute of it, which can seem surprising until we think back and realize that the moments when we're pushing ourselves often aren't very comfortable. But in the end, the triumph of achieving something we worked hard at vastly overshadows the effort and pain needed to get there.

While early work referred to flow as being a state, in large part because of the language surrounding highly focused states of consciousness like mindfulness or hypnosis, flow is more aptly characterized as an experience. As John Dewey (1934) wrote:

Jef J. J. van den Hout and O. C. Davis, *Team Flow*, SpringerBriefs in Well-Being and Quality of Life Research, https://doi.org/10.1007/978-3-030-27871-7_1

> Experience is the result, the sign, and the reward of that interaction of organism and environment which, when it is carried to the full, is a transformation of interaction into participation and communication. (p. 22)

In a state, we separate ourselves from much of our environment, or we become so engrossed in it that we lose the boundary between it and ourselves. In flow, however, we retain our individuality while simultaneously interacting with our environment, both changing it and being changed by it through a complex system of transactions that no model has come close to quantifying. As described by Alexey Leontiev (1994), the act of experiencing is one of creating meaning, and while the construct of flow does not have any inherent meaning, the context in which one experiences flow allows it to create meaning. In this we experience the environment acting upon us in an intricate way even as we are applying our uniqueness to act upon the world. By deliberately engaging in the process of being within our microcosms, we experience a meaningful event in which we both create and are created (cf. Vasilyuk, 1991).

As such, it is important to start our discussion of flow with the understanding that it is an experience that is made meaningful through the effort that is applied in a specific context. That is, flow is not necessarily a positive experience, but rather an *engaged* experience that we find meaningful and about which we feel positive afterwards. That positivity may or may not be of the kind we experience when sampling fine food, receiving a reward, or embracing a loved one. Rather, flow has an existential component, the experience of which often resonates with our personal *raison d'etre* because of its autotelic nature (something we explore below).

It is no surprise, then, that team flow is also a meaningful experience, and one that requires a clear understanding of why the team exists. For a team to be capable of experiencing flow, it must have a purpose and it must exist to interact with the environment in ways that allow it to create things individuals never could. Indeed, the world must change (and almost certainly for the better!) for having *this team* apply its unique mark to the canvas of its environment.

Like any experience, we can view flow through three different experiential dimensions: emotion (pleasure), relation (meaning), and control (effort). Fundamentally, flow is the application of one's efforts in ways that will yield pleasure once we have absorbed ourselves in the deliberate attempt to overcome challenges we have established for ourselves (cf. Leontiev, Osin, Dosumova, & Rzaeva, 2019). When our interactions with the environment afford the opportunity to create meaning with and through our flow experiences, we have not just flow, but *engagement*. This elusive construct is highly sought after by companies because it correlates strongly with high performance. Engagement is what emerges when we are achieving something that exceeds our individual nature (transcending the self!) to increase the order and complexity of the world in valuable ways. Or should we say, since we are discussing flow in a professional context, in *profitable ways*.

One of the best parts about flow experiences is that they can happen in any activity. Though they most commonly occur in work and leisure, any task to which the characteristics of flow can be applied can produce a flow experience, even eating! Flow can occur in any reasonable span of time, provided one has the opportunity to become sufficiently immersed in the activity. Flow can happen for individuals, for dyads, and for teams, and has slightly different characteristics in each context, but the results are fantastic every time. That said, even though flow can be made to happen anywhere and anytime, it remains somewhat elusive. And that's exactly why we're writing this book! Research, including our own, shows that there are ways to create more opportunities for experiencing flow, and we are eager to share them with you.

Flow was originally discovered by Mihály Csíkszentmihályi in the early 1960s, when he was working on his doctoral dissertation on creativity. He was originally studying artists, and was particularly interested by what motivated some of them to keep doing art even though the pay was low. He found that some of them were motivated to engage in art for its own sake, such that the process of creating the pieces was sufficiently enjoyable and meaningful in and of itself to make the endeavor worthwhile. Curious about this phenomenon, Csíkszentmihályi discovered that this intrinsic motivation appeared across a wide range of hobbies and professions, and as he interviewed people and conducted experiments over the next 10 years, several interviewees referred to the experience as being carried along by a current, and at least one of whom referred to the activity as operating in a "flow" (though entirely different from the concept of "going with the flow"), and so the concept of flow was born.

> The mystique of rock climbing is climbing; you get to the top of a rock glad it's over but really wishing it would go on forever. The justification of climbing is climbing, like the justification of poetry is writing; you don't conquer anything except things in yourself…
>
> The act of writing justifies poetry. Climbing is the same: recognizing that you are in flow. The purpose of the flow is to keep on flowing, not looking for a peak or utopia but staying in the flow. It is not a moving up but a continuous flowing; you move up only to keep the flow going. There is no possible reason for climbing except the climbing itself; it is a self-communication.
>
> A rock climber (Csíkszentmihályi, 1975, p. 48)

1.2 Flow in Business Teams

Just as flow experiences incite people to improve at their hobbies, so too does flow lead to the pursuit of higher skill levels in career-related activities. In fact, research shows that flow happens most frequently at work (Csíkszentmihályi, 1997), and that higher performance tends to result. As such, flow experiences are extremely valuable to companies, because the more employees experience flow, the more they will love their jobs, perform well, come up with more creative solutions, and put their all into their work (Bryce & Haworth, 2002; Csíkszentmihályi & LeFevre, 1989; Fredrickson, 2001; Hektner, Schmidt & Csíkszentmihályi, 2007; Massimini & Carli, 1988). The benefits of flow at work can hardly be overstated. When people experience flow at work, they experience their jobs more as meaningful callings, and are willing to go above and beyond their job descriptions. In addition, they are more likely to develop their skills, becoming better able to perform complex tasks and create value. This is great for the people doing the work, as they derive both pleasure and meaning from what they do, and great for the company (for obvious reasons). This win-win for the company and its employees makes flow a valuable investment.

1.3 Toward an Understanding of Team Flow

For businesses to stay successful and innovative, the tasks that must be completed by their workers have become ever more complex, and many businesses now find teamwork essential. Thankfully, flow is as possible for teams as it is for individuals. Even though *team flow* is a far more complex phenomenon, its benefits are spectacular. Have you ever watched a team that is fluidly synchronized in its execution of a complex task, be it a performance team, a sports team, or a business team? Every member knows where they are supposed to be, what they are supposed to be doing, and is performing their function flawlessly in perfect coordination with the rest of the team. This team flow experience and its accompanying benefits are experienced both at the individual and at the group level, creating feelings of positivity, connection, accomplishment, mastery, and meaning. In businesses, team flow increases an employee's connection and loyalty to the team, and thus to the company in which the team operates.

There will be a desire to reconvene with the team over and over again to have these great experiences of doing valuable work, which means that the synergistic gestalt of the whole team's discretionary efforts as well as those of each member will be in service of the company and its goals.

Thus, not only is flow an incredibly positive experience for individuals and teams, it is also meaningful, promotes mastery, and leads to high performance, which makes it profitable for individuals, teams, and businesses.

1.4 Contribution

Our goal in writing this book is to make flow, and especially team flow, more accessible, so that more people will have more optimal experiences throughout their lives. We put special emphasis on business teams because people spend so much of their time at work and increasingly more of that time in teams. We have noticed that a large number of people anticipate team work as eagerly as they do dental work, and we want to show how being on a team can be not just a positive experience, but a fulfilling one. We have also seen many businesses try to create effective teams and fall flat on their faces, so we aim to delineate a clear set of guidelines for building a high-performing team. And for the teams that are already hitting high bars, we hope to launch them into the stratosphere.

1.5 What Lies Ahead

As you read through this book, you will learn what flow is and how to experience it at the individual level (Chap. 2). Then, we will explain how individual flow can be extended to the team level with a detailed look at the 11 elements of team flow (Chap. 3). Putting these elements together, we will show how to create an environment conducive to team flow and a context from which team flow can emerge (Chap. 4). We concede that creating team flow is difficult, in part because so many things can impede it. We will examine these possible impediments and learn how to troubleshoot them in Chap. 5. In Chap. 6, we broaden our view to look at how the team operates in the context of the organization, and specifically how the organization can inhibit or contribute to team flow. Putting it all together, we will detail the means and methods by which teams can create flow experiences and troubleshoot any problems that arise in Chap. 7. Finally, we will speculate on the future of teamwork in Chap. 8.

TEAM: Together, Everyone Achieves More!

References

Bryce, J., & Haworth, J. (2002). Wellbeing and flow in sample of male and female office workers. *Leisure Studies, 21*(3–4), 249–263. https://doi.org/10.1080/02614360210000306 87.

Csíkszentmihályi, M. (1975). *Beyond boredom and anxiety*. San Francisco, CA: Jossey-Bass Publishers.

Csíkszentmihályi, M. (1997). *Finding flow: The psychology of engagement with everyday life*. New York: Basic Books.

Csíkszentmihályi, M., & LeFevre, J. (1989). Optimal experience in work and leisure. *Journal of Personality and Social Psychology, 56*(5), 815–822.

Dewey, J. (1934). *Art as experience*. New York: Perigee.

Fredrickson, B. L. (2001). The role of positive emotions in positive psychology: The broaden-and-build theory of positive emotions. *American Psychologist, 56*(3), 218–226.

Hektner, J. M., Schmidt, J. A., & Csíkszentmihályi, M. (2007). *Experience sampling method: Measuring the quality of everyday life*. Thousand Oaks, CA: Sage Publications Inc.

Leontiev, A. N. (1994). *Filosofiya psikhologii* [Philosophy of Psychology]. Moscow: Moscow State University.

Leontiev, D., Osin, E., Dosumova, S., & Rzaeva, F. (2019). *Experiences in activity: Theoretical model, assessment, and empirical evidence*. Toronto, Canada: Poster presented at the meeting of the American Educational Research Association.

Massimini, F., & Carli, M. (1988). The systematic measurement of flow in daily experience. In M. Csíkszentmihályi & I. S. Csíkszentmihályi (Eds.), *Optimal experience: Psychological studies of flow in consciousness*. Cambridge: Cambridge University Press.

Vasilyuk, F. (1991). *The psychology of experiencing: The resolution of life's critical situations*. New York: Harvester Wheatsheaf.

Chapter 2
The Individual Flow Experience in the Context of Teams

As we now have a broad understanding of the phenomenon of flow, it is time to delve deeper into the literature on *how* one comes to experience flow. Which prerequisites enable us to experience flow and what are the characteristics of workplace flow experiences?

2.1 Flow Theory in the Context of Work Teams

Since people spend much of their time at their jobs, work becomes one of the primary means of developing and expressing oneself. Many people choose career paths that reflect their talents and values, seeking meaning and self-actualization. To succeed in those careers, they study (often for years), find employment, and continue to train throughout their lives. They build skills, tackle challenges, and at their peak they go on and achieve a level of creative production consistent with Maslovian self-actualization. Such high levels can be attained in almost any profession, and are often punctuated by flow experiences that reflect increasing levels of mastery, productivity, meaning, and creativity.

Many are thus intrinsically motivated to engage with the work they have chosen. Even those who don't find their jobs inherently motivating look for ways to make work worth doing for its own sake. It could be trying to do a simple job in a new and challenging way, or with fewer resources, or more quickly, and so on. When people are intrinsically motivated to do their jobs, they are more loyal to their company and manager, more energetic in their work, and more willing to put in the hours and the effort required to excel. They volunteer, they go the extra mile, and they seek out challenges. In doing so, they improve their ability to create value and come up with alternative and creative solutions. Pursuing mastery, they push the boundaries of what they (and therefore the company) can produce, often reaching tangible (and valuable) milestones as they chase the horizon.

Jef J. J. van den Hout and O. C. Davis, *Team Flow*, SpringerBriefs in Well-Being and Quality of Life Research, https://doi.org/10.1007/978-3-030-27871-7_2

Flow is the conduit through which all of these processes occur, and thus finding flow is the holy grail of business success for individual employees, teams, and companies.

2.2 The Task Flow Experience

Flow can be described as the enjoyable experience of having one's attention completely absorbed in the present moment while working on the challenges at hand. While experiencing flow, all of one's thoughts, feelings, wishes, and actions are in harmony, and the activity itself is perceived to be intrinsically rewarding (Bryce & Haworth, 2002; Csíkszentmihályi, 1990, 1997; Nakamura & Csíkszentmihályi, 2009). There is a sudden and enjoyable merging of action and awareness, such that actions follow one upon the other spontaneously and unselfconsciously (Rathunde & Csíkszentmihályi, 2006).

Flow is likely to occur when people perceive a challenge or an opportunity for action that meets (or slightly exceeds) their skill level, which promotes deeper engagement (Abuhamdeh & Csíkszentmihályi, 2009; Asakawa, 2004; Csíkszentmihályi, 1990; Moneta & Csíkszentmihályi, 1996). At that level of challenge relative to skill, individuals stretch their abilities, which is likely to enhance their skills and increase their self-efficacy and personal complexity (Csíkszentmihályi & LeFevre, 1989; cf. Ullén et al., 2012). The effects of balancing skill level and challenge are clearly visualized in Fig. 2.1. When one lacks the appropriate skills to meet a challenge, feelings of anxiety can result, whereas non-challenging tasks can be very relaxing (and not at all engaging) for highly skilled people. When people focus on a challenging activity and are intrinsically

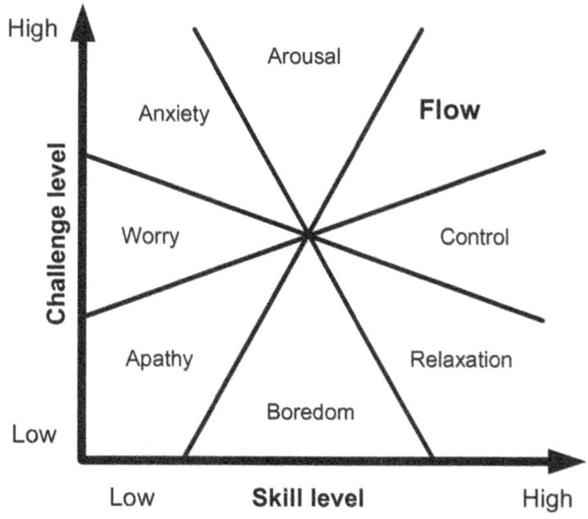

Fig. 2.1 Challenge-skill balance required for flow (Csíkszentmihályi, 1997)

motivated (both typical elements of a flow experience), likely outcomes include work of higher creative value, better performance, and a desire to engage in the activity again in the future (Csíkszentmihályi, 1997; Landhäußer & Keller, 2012).

Csíkszentmihályi used nine key elements to characterize flow (Csíkszentmihályi, 1990; Nakamura & Csíkszentmihályi, 2009). Three of them have been identified as readily-generated prerequisites for experiencing flow:

1. Clear proximal goals at every stage of the activity
2. Clear and relatively immediate feedback on one's actions and progress (see Amabile & Kramer, 2011, for the value and importance of immediate feedback)
3. Opportunities for action perceived as challenging, meaning that the difficulty of the activity is well-matched to the skill level of the actor

With these prerequisites in place, it is easier for people to experience the six subjective states associated with flow, namely:

4. Intense and focused concentration on the activity, without any distractions, such that all of one's thoughts, effort, and attention are directed at the task at hand
5. A sense that one has control over the situation without the fear of failure, such that one can deal with any reasonable permutation of the current situation because one knows how to respond to whatever may happen next (Hektner et al., 2007; Jackson & Eklund, 2004)
6. A sense of *autotelicity*, meaning that the activity is done for its own sake or is intrinsically rewarding, such that the stated goal tends to be an excuse for engaging in the process. Autotelic people are primed for opportunities to turn almost any situation into an opportunity for engagement (Csíkszentmihályi, 1975; Tse, Lau, Perlman, & McLaughlin, 2018)
7. The loss of reflective self-consciousness, such that all concern for the self disappears and the person perceives a sense of unity with the activity (i.e., loss of awareness of oneself as a social actor)
8. A distorted sense of the passage of time (Csíkszentmihályi, 1990, 1996)
9. A merging of action and awareness, meaning that one's involvement in an activity is so intense that the correct behavior becomes spontaneous and automatic.

Among the primary and most critical elements of flow is autotelicity (Greek: autos [self] + telos [goal]): doing the activity for its own sake, such that the goal tends to be merely an excuse for engaging in the activity. The stated goal of a mountain climber is to reach the top, but in a flow experience, the climber climbs just to climb. Likewise, factory workers experiencing flow may set themselves challenges for the sheer love of the exertion required to complete them. As such, the biggest difference between the experience of success and the experience of flow is that the latter involves an activity that one is intrinsically motivated to engage in. One performs the task for the sheer joy of doing so, because the task is meaningful, allows for authentic self-expression, or enables one to experience oneself more fully, or some combination thereof. Due to its autotelic nature, flow is necessarily an experience that expresses one's uniqueness and is thus more meaningful.

The second element of flow is an objective (or set of objectives) that is clear and readily understood at every stage of the endeavor. At all times, actors know the goal [s] of their current actions, and how each [sub-]goal contributes to the overarching objectives. In a game of darts, the long-term goal is to win the match, but there are also the more proximal goals of winning each set, each of the 3 legs in each set, and to throw out 501 points in each leg. But every dart is its own throw, and the thrower gets clear feedback about how well each throw serves the higher-order goals of the leg, set, and match.

The third element of flow is *clear and timely feedback about one's actions that provides an indicator of progress towards the [sub-]goals.* It is not enough just to have a goal—actors must see their progress and know at every stage that the goal remains achievable. A computer programmer, for instance, often spends a lot of time debugging, and many a coder has experienced flow in the process (and some very triumphant moments cleaning up complex code). One of the reasons for this is not just the clear goal (a working program), but error indicators either built into the development environment, program, and/or compiler that provide feedback on how the code is developing. After a programmer sets the code and tests/compiles it, the system will respond with either the correct result or a clue as to why the expected outcome has not appeared. Often, those clues lead into the kind of detective mystery that might stump Sherlock Holmes, since even if the solution is elementary, finding the problem rarely is. Coders often must create scenarios that prompt the program to fail in ways that provide clues to errors in the code, which is deliberately cultivating the feedback they need.

The fourth element of flow is *a challenge or opportunity commensurate with the actor's skill level.* Even with a clear goal and a way of knowing whether one is making reasonable progress, easy activities are still pretty boring. Most business-people, for instance, don't enjoy submitting their monthly expense reports, in large part because it is tedious (i.e., not challenging). We're not offering this as a solution, but we would wager that expense reports would be a lot more fun if they had to be completed accurately in a short span of time (among other important contextual additions that would effectively gamify the process). The difference between such an activity being enjoyable and being stressful depends very much upon the level of challenge that the task presents. For a person typing at the average speed of 40 words per minute who has to enter 100 items into an expense report, a 3-min time limit is insane, while a time limit of 20–25 min is tough-but-doable. This aspect, being challenging but achievable, is critical to flow. Impossible challenges are distressing and tasks with no challenge at all are tedious. There is a sweet spot of challenge relative to skill in which the former is at or slightly above the latter, but in which both are above the average level defined by the actor's range of capabilities. Although it might seem optimal to have a person tackle a challenge that requires the utmost of their skills, people don't always have the space, resources, or energy to engage in such a task. As long as the challenge is great enough that applying the required skill is effortful, the activity can be considered conducive to flow.

The fifth element of flow is *a sense that one can handle the situation and thus need not fear failure.* It is not that failure is impossible in such a case, for the presence of a high level of challenge often implies the very real possibility of failure, but rather that one is focused on achieving the goal and confident that one has the wherewithal to succeed. An attorney in flow arguing a challenging case in court is focused entirely upon making good arguments and applying all of their legal knowledge and skills to the task. There is no room in that process to consider the possibility of failure, as it would detract from providing the highest level of legal service. Though the attorney cannot know exactly how the case will proceed, they feel confident they can handle whatever happens next.

The fifth characteristic of flow is intense focus that excludes all distractions. The full measure of one's thoughts, efforts, and attention are applied only to the current activity. A human resources manager reviewing resumes would only be able to experience flow if they focused completely on the pile of letters in front of them. There would be no attention to spare for a ringing phone, no thoughts about what is for lunch, not even concern about the deadline for hiring someone. Finding the right candidate(s) in that stack of resumes is that manager's first, last, and only concern throughout their flow experience.

The seventh element is a merger of action and awareness consistent with such a deep involvement in the activity that one's actions feel spontaneous and automatic. A hairdresser, for example, can often envision the end result before making the first cut. While working, the stylist responds fluidly to the changing head of hair, incorporating even the motions of the client into the movements needed to shape the hair to the desired end. The focused hairdresser thinks only of the styling, the tools in hand, the shaping motions required, and the development of a look. The act of creation feels effortless, in spite of the significant amounts of thought and energy going into it.

The eight element is *a loss of reflective self-consciousness.* One's focus becomes so deep, and the action so engrossing, that one forgets to think of oneself as the actor. One effectively becomes the act rather than the agent. A filing clerk in flow sees only the files, their destinations, and the motions needed to get them there. The clerk loses the sense of "I am doing this." Consider that when you are reading a book that you enjoy, you tend to forget that you are "doing reading" and simply follow along with the story.

The ninth element is *a distorted sense of the passage of time.* For instance, the physical therapist analyzing a client's motion reviews each intricate piece of it with a practiced eye. The focus and expertise required to break down the client's action can make a quick and simple movement seem to take place in slow motion. By contrast, an accountant engrossed in the preparation of a tax return prepares it swiftly and fluidly despite its complexity, but such smoothness of action can conceal the actual amount of time that elapses during the process. During a flow experience, time subjectively passes at whatever rate the activity requires, stretching or compressing the experience of minutes and hours as needed.

Three of the subjective elements of flow (total concentration, sense of control, and autotelic experience) are easier to recall than the others and could function as anchors that, once established, are readily accessible for instantiating an experience that is more conducive to the emergence of flow.

With regard to total concentration, anyone can achieve a certain level of concentration with conscious effort, practice, and/or training. People are also quite capable of excluding any distractions from their work environment that might damage their concentration on the task at hand. Therefore, complete concentration on the present moment (where distractions are excluded from consciousness) can also be seen as a prerequisite of the flow experience.

The same applies to the sense of control. When one is in control of the situation, one is not concerned about failing because one knows how to respond to any situation, stimulus, or event relating to the task environment that could possibly arise and increase the risk of failure. A sense of control also entails a person choosing to perform to the best of their abilities even as they accept that factors beyond their control may affect the outcome of their efforts. This view implies that situations are determined by the individual's actions and their reactions to external influences, which in turn implies that the individual is sufficiently in control of the self relative to the situation/environment.

People recall the experience of an activity as intrinsically rewarding after finding the activity highly rewarding/engaging and meaningful. Recognizing the autotelic nature of an activity/experience can also be considered a prerequisite of flow, as people who know what they love to do can more readily choose to engage in that activity just for the sake of doing it. Autotelic goals fit and feed the identity of the people that choose them in a way that provides purpose and meaning. For instance, one can choose to play a specific instrument, or a specific sport, or a specific position (task or role) in a team, because that specific selection is resonant with their identities.

The three remaining elements (merging of action and awareness, loss of reflective self-consciousness, and distortion of temporal experience) usually do not serve as prerequisites of the flow experience. Trying to create these elements of the flow experience consciously tends to backfire (Csíkszentmihályi, 1997; Gardner, Csíkszentmihályi, & Damon, 2001). Because of their emergent nature, these elements are truly inherent characteristics of the flow experience.

To summarize, there are nine elements that typify the flow experience, and are usually present in full an intense flow experience occurs. Three of these elements are prerequisites for the flow experience and depend on the external task environment, three others bridge the gap between the external environment and the internal experience of the subject and can be seen as prerequisites and characteristics, and the last three are purely internal and are strong indicators of whether flow is being experienced (Table 2.1).

Table 2.1 Classification of the nine elements of flow

Prerequisites		*Elements that need to be created, or at least present, in the work environment*	(1) Challenges matched to skill level
			(2) Clear proximal goal(s)
			(3) Clear and immediate feedback
	Characteristics	*Elements that can be influenced (like prerequisites) but are also indicative of flow (like characteristics)*	(4) Total concentration; Oblivious to distraction
			(5) Sense of control; No fear of failure
			(6) Intrinsic motivation; Autotelic experience
		Elements describing internal states that only occur during flow experiences	(7) Merging of action and awareness
			(8) Loss of reflective self-consciousness
			(9) Distorted experience of time passing

2.3 The Downsides of Flow

Flow is a highly desirable experience that is worth promoting by ensuring its prerequisites are present in work contexts. Although we have seen that flow has may positive aspects, research shows that there are also some downsides to the flow experience. The definition of flow reveals that people will incur great costs to achieve it because the experience is so enjoyable (Csíkszentmihályi, 1990). This urge can make people expend too much time, money, and physical effort, and cause them to disregard other goals, jeopardizing their psychological growth (Schüler, 2012). Schüler (2012) goes on to explain that each of the conditions of flow has a particular downside. The loss of reflective self, for example, could lead one to neglect long-term goals and personal values, and complete concentration on the task at hand could cause one to exclude situationally irrelevant but still vitally important information, such as social cues about the inappropriateness of one's behavior, or forgetting time in the context of time-sensitive tasks. In short, flow experiences can potentially lead to short-sighted, self-centered, and/or high-risk behaviors. We should be aware of these negative consequences when conceptualizing team flow.

Sinking into Flow Here are step-by-step instructions to guide you from sitting down at your desk into the optimal work experience using the elements of individual flow:

1. Pick up an activity, task or role find enjoyable, important and/or valuable.
2. Set yourself a clear final objective and as many proximal goals as necessary in each step of performing your task.
3. Be sure to set your goals so that they are challenging without becoming frustrating, but be prepared to surprise yourself with what you can do.
4. Identify/Create mechanisms for receiving just enough direct and constructive feedback to keep you on task and aware of your progress.
5. Exclude distractions as best you can and apply yourself to concentrating fully on the task at hand.
6. Recognize that you are in control of this situation and prepared for eventualities. You have the skills. You set the challenge.
7. Then, give yourself over to the activity and become one with it…
8. …you might start to act spontaneously now, and…
9. …lose your sense of time.

When you emerge from the task, you will realise you were in flow.

If your personal task/role is part of a team collaboration, go over steps 1 through 6 together with your teammates. Ask them to help you.

Schüler (2012) further states that flow experiences show some overlap with addiction, referencing Csíkszentmihályi's statement that "when a person becomes so dependent on the ability to control an enjoyable activity that (s)he cannot pay attention to anything else, then he loses the ultimate control: the freedom to determine the content of consciousness" (Csíkszentmihályi, 1990, p. 62). In our view, the experience of flow is never the reason people get addicted, but it may serve as a potentially harmful coping mechanism for people who are dealing with psychological difficulties with any number and combination of physical, mental, circumstantial, and emotional factors. Therefore, addiction should not be considered a negative aspect of flow, nor does addiction need to be considered when applying the conceptualization of flow to the context of work teams. It is enough that people be made aware that flow-seeking behavior may be indicative of an underlying psychological disturbance, especially when undertaken to excess.

To experience flow, people seek out significant challenges to test their skills against. Naturally, these challenging activities are often accompanied by significant risk (Rheinberg, 1991). Similar points have been made in other studies over the years, suggesting that the loss of reflective self may impair risk-assessment skills and that the desire to have more (inherently pleasurable) flow experiences may increase risk acceptance (Rheinberg, 1991; Sato, 1988; Schüler & Pfenninger, 2011). When considering these previous findings, it is important to remember that in many activities risk-taking is appropriate, if not downright necessary, behavior. Most businesses stand to benefit enormously from promoting flow in their teams and individual employees, even if it does incur some measure of risk. Mitigating that risk is best accomplished within the team, by keeping lines of communication open, staying aware of what each team member is doing, and flagging unacceptable risks before they lead to catastrophe. Even acceptable risks will occasionally lead to failure, but failure and the ability to tolerate and learn from failure are what allows team members to operate at the peak of their abilities while at the same time building up their skills.

One final point is that flow can be experienced in any kind of activity (Csíkszentmihályi, 1990), even those undertaken in antisocial contexts (Csíkszentmihályi & Rathunde, 1993), like aggression, violence, and crime. Whether these experiences are truly satisfying and/or gratifying is questionable. Most of these behaviors and their likely underlying causes seemingly have little to do with "doing something for its own sake," and more with significant psychological and socio-economic factors such as emotional disturbance, poverty, mental illness, and drifting social norms in small groups. Flow-seeking may play a role, but that does not inherently make it more harmful than basic pleasure-seeking.

Overall, we think that flow should be considered a positive experience. It is a gratifying, holistic experience arising from engaging in a challenging-but-doable activity. When flow is experienced in an unhealthy context or while engaged in a damaging activity, there will likely be negative consequences. Though these consequences may be severe, ranging from feelings of regret to real and lasting damage to people's lives, flow is at worst a contributing factor, and never a direct cause. On the individual level, these downsides can be mitigated through awareness and vigilance. In the context of team flow, such mitigation is likely to be much more effective, since there is a whole team of people ensuring that each team member keeps contributing to the team's overall objectives.

> There was confidence in the group itself after the performance at Pinkpop…At Oerol it was more the awareness of each [band member's] uplifting in it…that is the ultimate that you experience that together with the audience. Otherwise it is a sort of separate thing…you give it as a group and then you experience it either as a group or individually with the audience and then separate from the group, but sometimes it is all one thing. [The concert at] Heerlen was also fuckin' amazing by the way – that was also insane and we were one with the audience.
>
> Rapper ReaZun of the Kyteman Hip Hop Orchestra (2009)

2.4 Overview of Extant Research on Interpersonal Flow at Work

Few studies have been conducted into flow experiences among team members of professional teams at work. An overview of the most important research that has been done on the subject is provided here to help the reader understand the conceptualization of team flow in a business context.

One of the pioneers in the area of shared flow experiences is Keith Sawyer, who defined group flow as "a collective state that occurs when a group is performing at the peak of its abilities" (Sawyer, 2003, p. 167). His work is mainly based on groups in the performing arts, such as jazz bands and improvisational theatre companies. Sawyer (2007) conducted qualitative research to ascertain that group flow emerges in contexts where ten key flow-enabling conditions are present: (1) the group's goal, (2) close listening, (3) complete concentration, (4) being in control, (5) blending egos, (6) equal participation, (7) familiarity, (8) communication, (9) moving it forward, (10) the potential for failure. Sawyer (2006) defines group flow as a property of the group as a collective unit:

> Group flow is not the same thing as the psychological state of flow. It depends on interaction among performers and it emerges from this process. The group can be in flow even when the members are not; or the group might not be in flow even when the members are. The study of group flow thus requires a fundamentally social psychology and must proceed by examining the interactional dynamics among members during performance (p. 159).

While we concede that a group can attain a 'collective state of mind,' Sawyer's view that group flow allows for individuals not to experience flow is questionable in light of studies on athletes experiencing flow in group sports (cf. Jackson & Eklund, 2004; Jackson, Kimiecik, Ford, & Marsh, 1998; Jackson & Csíkszentmihályi, 1999; Russell, 2001), as well as a report on flow in motorcycle gangs in Japan (Sato, 1988). These studies all show that it is the individual who experiences flow as a function of participating in a group activity and suggest a contagion effect in which the flow experiences of some infect the others until all of the individuals experience flow in a way that aggregates to a team-level phenomenon (cf. Bakker, 2005; Culbertson, Fullagar, Simmons & Zhu, 2015).

Based on the work of Sawyer, Armstrong (2008) carried out a study on a small group of students in a mathematics classroom. In this study, they found that creating small groups is necessary to reach an experience of group flow. Armstrong found that a balance between the number of shared structures and the nature of the collective goal (extrinsic or intrinsic) supports the achievement of group flow. He stated that "the more extrinsic the goal, the more shared structures are required to ensure that the group is able to achieve this goal in an effective manner" (Armstrong, 2008, p. 103). Approaching this idea from the other side, he goes on to say "when the group is problem-finding—then fewer shared structures are required, and the group's performance can be more exploratory and improvisational." (Armstrong, 2008, p. 103) Moreover, he argues that as group flow emerges, so do other indicative physical behaviors such as posture, positioning, gestures, and facial expression, as well as verbal indicators such as modulated tone of voice, echoing, repeating words or phrases, altered rates of speech, and fragmentation of speech. Team members also start synchronizing their actions. This indicates that a collective flow experience can be observed physically, based on the behavior of the team members. As they synchronize their actions, their collective awareness merges with their coordinated actions. This synergy of actions will produce the experience of moving forward together (cf. Sawyer, 2007).

Quinn (2005) defines collective flow as the experience of people "moving together toward shared or complementary goals, adjusting in real time to each other's expectations, needs, and contributions, and learning how others work and how to interact effectively along the way" (p. 637). In his doctoral thesis, Quinn (2003) identified three key differences between individual and collective flow, which he described as additional antecedents for the experience of collective flow. They are (1) the coordination of activities between members of the collective through both cognitive and affective processes, (2) a collective goal that takes precedence over the other elements of the collective structure, and (3) the need for comparable levels of skill. To obtain this collective flow he stated that all original elements of flow and the three team antecedents have to be present.

Walker (2010) came up with another way to describe the shared flow experience. He coined the term social flow to refer to the experience of flow in a social context and argues that social flow must be similar to solitary flow because, in order to experience the former, all the conditions for the latter must be met first. On the other hand, social and solitary flow may be qualitatively different experiences. "After all, people act, think, and feel qualitatively differently within a group than they do by themselves (cf. Allport, 1954; Asch, 1956; Latane & Darley, 1968; Lewin, 1952; Milgram, 1965; Zimbardo, 1969)" (Walker, 2010, p. 4). Walker (2010) describes a specific type of social flow, interactive social flow, which occurs when team members interact intensively in situations where they are highly interdependent and must cooperate to coordinate their performances within the established team, possibly serving as agents of flow for each other. Walker (2010) describes this form of flow as mutual and reciprocal and states that "interactive social flow can be easily seen in highly cohesive teams, in teams where there is agreement on goals, procedures, roles, and patterns of interpersonal relations and the competency of team members is uniformly high (Hackman, Wageman, Ruddy, & Ray, 2000)" (p. 4). Moreover, he found that when the level of social interdependence was manipulated, participants in highly interdependent teams reported more joy in flow than individuals performing less interdependently. As such, teams that work more closely together are likely to experience more joy in their flow experiences. But, the reasons for this requires more research. One of the factors which could lead to this more enjoyable experience is the contagious nature of emotions, also called the contagion effect (as described earlier). But, the effect can also be attributed to the fact that people in a team setting are required to work together intensively. Walker (2010) showed this in his experiment by making participants work together by passing balls behind their backs or under their legs in a manner that required high levels of coordination. Based on his findings, Walker (2010) also considered whether social flow experiences might be subject to some emergent collective phenomenon that potentially makes them more intense than the individual flow experiences of everyone involved.

Snow (2010) introduces the term interpersonal flow in the work context as: "The state in which two people are mutually engaged in a shared activity such that both individuals would describe their experience as: (a) having their perspective broadened by the other person, (b) feeling a shared sense of identity, (c) not feeling self-conscious with each other, (d) not worrying about what outsiders think, (e) having total concentration on the shared activity, (f) feeling able to respond almost instantly to presenting situations as a pair, (g) time passing more quickly or slowly than usual, and (h) enjoyable and intrinsically rewarding. (p. 2). The occurrence of interpersonal flow determined the exchange of knowledge within the group, while the focus of individual team members on their tasks predicted the absorption of knowledge available in the group. These two predictive elements could help members achieve a smoother collaboration and even a potential collective flow experience.

Zumeta, Basabe, Włodarczyk, Bobowik, and Páez (2016) conceptualized the measure of collective flow based on their shared flow scale, which measured flow in the "we-form". They measured the shared flow experience during collective drumming (Tamborrada) sessions and found that these gatherings stimulate shared flow experiences and promote personal wellbeing as well social cohesion. Their findings show that shared flow mediates the effect between involvement (intensity, satisfaction, involvement, and pride) on collective efficacy and wellbeing, social integration, and identity fusion.

An exploratory study carried out by Magyaròdi and Oláh (2015) found that social activities involving work and sports are the most likely to induce flow experiences. This study concludes that interpersonal flow experiences require a high level of perceived challenge. Magyaròdi and Oláh (2015) identified other interpersonal flow enablers as well: the level of cooperation, the immediateness and clarity of feedback, and the perceived level of skill. It is interesting to see that some of these elements show a clear resemblance to those of the individual flow experience.

Other studies that identified elements which contributed to the occurrence of shared flow experiences include that of Keith et al. (2014). Their study on teams participating in collaborative video gaming emphasizes the importance of mutual commitment to the conceptualization of team flow and defines team flow as a situation that "occurs when a team is able to become completely immersed in an interdependent task that members are intrinsically gratified together" (p. 2). They argue that team flow is affected more by the nature of the task itself (i.e., enjoyment, time dissociation, control, curiosity, immersion, communication) than by team cohesion, which is determined by how team members evaluate each other (i.e. pride, unity and social relations). Also, personal resources (i.e., self-efficacy beliefs) and organizational resources (i.e., social support and clear goals) are found to facilitate work-related flow among secondary school teachers (Salanova et al., 2006). In their study, Salanova et al. defined flow as being a function of work absorption, work enjoyment, and intrinsic work motivation. In turn, these flow experiences had a positive influence on those resources, which provides support for the conceptualization of flow as a virtuous cycle. In a study that elaborates on their earlier work, Salanova, Rodríguez-Sánchez, Schaufeli, & Cifre (2014) extended Csíkszentmihályi's (1975, 1990) flow model to the group level (work groups) by including collective efficacy beliefs as a predictor of collective flow. They found a virtuous cycle in which collective efficacy beliefs predict collective flow over time, and that in turn collective flow predicts collective efficacy.

One of the latest conceptualizations of team flow comes from Mosek (2017). In an attempt to explain the nature of successful performance in sports teams, Mosek developed a team flow model that includes 14 elements. These 14 elements lie along two general dimensions. The first general dimension is based on the work of Mihály Csíkszentmihályi and contains seven elements of team flow, each of which is essentially an element of individual flow considered from the perspective of a team. The second main dimension comprises seven unique team flow elements, which were identified during a study among athletes and their coaches. These unique team flow elements are: game plan, team optimal arousal, coaching style, team communication, team confidence, external factors, and team support. Mosek excluded two elements of Csíkszentmihályi's (1975, 1990) original flow model from his conceptualization of team flow: loss of self-consciousness and sense of control. According to Mosek, the loss of self-consciousness is more applicable in an individual context. He based this on the fact that no mention of self-consciousness or its absence was made in the interviews. He also excluded a sense of control from his conceptualization. Instead, he listed a sense of control under the element of confidence, as the emotions resulting from a sense of control include power, confidence, and calm. While the study's focus on sports teams and qualitative nature are not as conducive to describing team flow both in general and in the workplace, the additional parameters do suggest ways in which managers and teams can facilitate team flow experiences.

Whereas previous parts mostly included shared flow experiences as a phenomenon distinct from individual flow, there have also been some studies regarding the effects of collectively experiencing individual flow. Aubé et al. (2014) have studied the role of individual-level flow in work teams, testing the relationship between flow, team goal commitment and team performance among students working in a project management simulation. They found that flow was positively correlated to team performance and influenced by goal commitment and the level of information exchange. The same positive effects of individual flow on team performance were found when secondary school students played a collaborative game that merged digital and real-world elements (Admiraal, Huizenga, Akkerman, & Dam, 2011). But, the research done by Aubé et al. (2014) did not include a broad conceptualization of the flow experience in teams. Although Aubé et al. measured levels of individual flow, collective flow should be considered as something more than the sum of the individuals' flow experiences. One reason to assume so would be that in social situations flow shows contagion effects (Bakker, 2005; Bakker, Oerlemans, Demerouti, Slot, & Ali, 2011; Engeser & Schiepe-Tiska, 2012) and is derived from interdependent teamwork (Keith, Anderson, Dean, & Gaskin, 2014; Sawyer, 2006; Walker, 2010). This interdependence places additional prerequisites on the experience of flow, and is in line with the previously mentioned work by Sawyer (2003), Quinn (2005), Snow (2010) and Walker (2010). Based on these findings, managers should implement interventions that foster the flow experience in their teams while at the same time encouraging information exchange between team members.

Baumgartner (2015) also studied the relationship between individual flow and performance while engaging a small team of five in an airport simulation. Her findings contradicted earlier findings on performance and suggested that flow is harmful for performance when that performance requires adaptive responses. The most likely explanation for this is that in a climate where team members correct and coach each other as they pursue a common goal, this collective effort may cancel out the effect of 'losing oneself in one's personal task.' Thus, in order to preserve the flow experience at the individual and team levels during tasks that require adaptive responses, the team ensure that individuals can get "lost" in the team's dynamics as it completes the interactive tasks. For instance, in a study among talented Dutch soccer players, Bakker et al. (2011) showed that environmental resources, such as social support from the coach and performance feedback during the soccer game, correlated positively with performance measures. This was shown by the fact that flow at the team level was more prevalent when the match resulted in a draw or win than when the match resulted in a loss.

Van Schaik, Martin, and Vallance (2012) studied individual flow within an immersive virtual environment for collaborative learning, where participants were asked to work on a collective task. They found that flow conditions (challenge-skill balance, clarity of goals and feedback) mediated between task constraints (the complexity inherent in a presented problem) and learning experience. Their findings support the idea that flow conditions could be used to create collective learning activities. These findings are also supported by Macdonald et al. (2006), which found that the quality of the output of groups that report higher levels of individual flow during a group music composition task is rated significantly higher by post-graduate student teachers.

Finally, Heyne, Pavlas, and Salas (2011) set up an experiment with three-person teams that were asked to complete a complex problem-solving task. In the study, researchers assessed the aggregate level of individual flow, and the results showed a relationship between a team's flow experience and task performance and between its flow experience and the processes members engage in. This suggests that flow functions similarly in teams and individuals, with the understanding that teams are subject to additional considerations, specifically team communication, information sharing, and team member perceptions of teammate performance and effort. Heyne et al. (2011) support the idea of developing and testing a comprehensive measure of flow at the team level (cf. Salanova et al., 2014; Walker, 2010).

Overall, we can conclude that the awareness of interaction effects among people in relation to flow experiences is increasing, and that there is a growing tendency to measure and investigate flow at a collective level. Our intention to study team flow follows from the suggestion that collective flow ought to be studied more extensively and from a broader perspective. Our research subjects therefore include both the experiences of the individual (aggregated or otherwise) and the *context* in which they occur (Fisher, 2010; Salanova et al., 2014; Sawyer, 2006; Walker, 2010). As noted by Snow (2010), little work has been done on the dynamics of team flow experiences in the workplace outside the context of creative production. To remedy that, our focus here is on group flow experiences as they apply to work teams. This necessitates a more nuanced conception of team flow: one that includes a *definition*, its *elements* (including a description of how each element of individual flow is represented in the dynamics of the team), and its *benefits* (the consequences and outcomes of team flow experiences). To that end, Van den Hout (2016) reviewed the literature regarding flow at the individual and group levels and applies these findings to the context of work teams. From there, he distills a definition for team flow in the work context and presents a testable model of team flow that includes the elements of the team flow experience.

To present a structured overview of how the team flow model relates to the other conceptualizations of team flow (Interpersonal Flow, Group Flow, Social Flow, Team Flow and Individual Flow), we created a table which incorporates all other conceptualizations of team flow and links them to the team flow model created by Van den Hout (2016). That table can be found in the appendix. The next chapter will elaborate on the elements included in Van den Hout's (2016) model of team flow.

References

Abuhamdeh, S., & Csíkszentmihályi, M. (2009). Intrinsic and extrinsic motivational orientations in the competitive context: An examination of person–situation interactions. *Journal of Personality, 77*(5), 1615–1635.

Admiraal, W., Huizenga, J., Akkerman, S., & ten Dam, G. (2011). The concept of flow in collaborative gamebased learning. *Computers in Human Behavior, 27*(3), 1185–1194.

Allport, G. W. (1954). The historical background of modern social psychology. In G. Lindzey (Ed.), *Handbook of social psychology* (Vol. 1, pp. 3–56). Reading, MA: Addison-Wesley.

Amabile, T. M., & Kramer, S. J. (2011). *The progress principle: Using small wins to ignite joy, engagement, and creativity at work.* Boston, MA: Harvard Business Review Press.

Armstrong, A. C. (2008). The fragility of group flow: The experiences of two small groups in a middle school mathematics classroom. *The Journal of Mathematical Behavior, 27*(2), 101–115.

Asakawa, K. (2004). Flow experience and autotelic personality in Japanese college students: How do they experience challenges in daily life? *Journal of Happiness Studies, 5*(2), 123–154.

Asch, S. E. (1956). Studies of independence and conformity: A minority of one against a unanimous majority. *Psychological Monographs: General and Applied, 70,* 1–70.

Aubé, C., Brunelle, E., & Rousseau, V. (2014). Flow experience and team performance: The role of team goal commitment and information exchange. *Motivation and Emotion, 38*(1), 120–130.

Bakker, A. B. (2005). Flow among music teachers and their students: The crossover of peak experiences. *Journal of Vocational Behavior, 66*(1), 26–44.

Bakker, A. B., Oerlemans, W., Demerouti, E., Slot, B. B., & Ali, D. K. (2011). Flow and performance: A study among talented Dutch soccer players. *Psychology of Sport and Exercise, 12*(4), 442–450.

Baumgartner, J. (2015). *The influence of flow on standard and adaptive performance in teams*. Master's Thesis. Retrieved from https://etd.ohiolink.edu/.

Bryce, J., & Haworth, J. (2002). Wellbeing and flow in sample of male and female office workers. *Leisure Studies, 21*(3–4), 249–263. https://doi.org/10.1080/0261436021000030687.

Csíkszentmihályi, M. (1975). *Beyond boredom and anxiety*. San Francisco, CA: Jossey-Bass Publishers.

Csíkszentmihályi, M. (1990). *Flow: The psychology of optimal experience*. New York: Harper and Row.

Csíkszentmihályi, M. (1996). *Creativity: Flow and the psychology of discovery and invention*. New York: HarperCollins.

Csíkszentmihályi, M. (1997). *Finding flow: The psychology of engagement with everyday life*. New York: Basic Books.

Csíkszentmihályi, M., & LeFevre, J. (1989). Optimal experience in work and leisure. *Journal of Personality and Social Psychology, 56*(5), 815–822.

Csíkszentmihályi, M., & Rathunde, K. (1993). The measurement of flow in everyday life: Toward a theory of emergent motivation. In R. Dienstbier & J. E. Jacobs (Eds.), *Nebraska symposium on motivation, 1992, 40, Developmental perspectives on motivation* (pp. 57–97). Lincoln: University of Nebraska Press.

Culbertson, S. S., Fullagar, C. J., Simmons, M. J., & Zhu, M. (2015). Contagious flow: Antecedents and consequences of optimal experience in the classroom. *Journal of Management Education, 39*(3), 319–349.

Engeser, S., & Schiepe-Tiska, A. (2012). Historical lines and an overview of current research on flow. In S. Engeser (Ed.), *Advances in flow research* (pp. 1–22). New York: Springer.

Fisher, C. D. (2010). Happiness at work. *International Journal of Management Reviews, 12*(4), 384–412.

Gardner, H. E., Csíkszentmihályi, M., & Damon, W. (2001). *Good work: When excellence and ethics meet*. New York: Basic Books.

Hackman, J. R., Wageman, R., Ruddy, T. M., & Ray, C. R. (2000). Team effectiveness in theory and practice. In C. Cooper & E. A. Locke (Eds.), *Industrial and organizational psychology: Theory and practice* (pp. 109–129). Oxford: Blackwell.

Hektner, J. M., Schmidt, J. A., & Csíkszentmihályi, M. (2007). *Experience sampling method: Measuring the quality of everyday life*. Thousand Oaks, CA: Sage Publications Inc.

Heyne, K., Pavlas, D., & Salas, E. (2011). An investigation on the effects of flow state on team process and outcomes. *Proceedings of the Human Factors and Ergonomics Society Annual Meeting, 55*(1), 475–479.

Jackson, S. A., & Csikszentmihalyi, M. (1999). *Flow in sports*. Champaign, IL: Human Kinetics.

Jackson, S. A., & Eklund, R. C. (2004). *The flow scales manual*. Morgantown, WV: Fitness Information Technology.

Jackson, S. A., Kimiecik, J. C., Ford, S. K., & Marsh, H. W. (1998). Psychological correlates of flow in sport. *Journal of Sport & Exercise Psychology, 20*(4), 358–378.

Keith, M., Anderson, G., Dean, D. L., & Gaskin, J. (2014). The effects of team flow on performance: A video game experiment. In *Proceedings of SIGHCI 2014*. Paper 13. Retrieved from http://aisel.aisnet.org/sighci2014/13.

Landhäußer, A., & Keller, J. (2012). Flow and its affective, cognitive, and performance-related consequences. In S. Engeser (Ed.), *Advances in flow research* (pp. 65–85). New York: Springer.

Latane, B., & Darley, J. M. (1968). Group inhibition of bystander intervention in emergencies. *Journal of Personality and Social Psychology, 10*, 215–221.

Lewin, K. (1952). Group decision and social change. In G. E. Swanson, T. M. Newcomb, & E. L. Harley (Eds.), *Readings in social psychology* (pp. 459–473). New York: Holt.

MacDonald, R., Byrne, C., & Carlton, L. (2006). Creativity and flow in musical composition: An empirical investigation. *Psychology of Music, 34,* 292–306. https://doi.org/10.1177/0305735606064838.

Magyaródi, T., & Oláh, A. (2015). Flow Szinkronizáció Kérdőív: az optimális élmény mechanizmusának mérése társas interakciós helyzetekben. *Mentálhigiéné és Pszichoszomatika, 16*(3), 271–296.

Milgram, S. (1965). Some conditions of obedience and disobedience to authority. *Human Relations, 18,* 57–75.

Moneta, G. B., & Csíkszentmihályi, M. (1996). The effect of perceived challenges and skills on the quality of subjective experience. *Journal of Personality, 64*(2), 275–310.

Mosek, E. (2017). *Team flow: The missing piece in performance*. Doctoral dissertation: Victoria University.

Nakamura, J., & Csíkszentmihályi, M. (2009). Flow theory and research. In C. R. Snyder & S. J. Lopez (Eds.), *The Oxford handbook of positive psychology* (2nd ed., pp. 195–206). Oxford: Oxford University Press.

Quinn, R. W. (2003). *Nuclear weapons and daily deadlines: The energy and tension of flow in knowledge work*. Unpublished doctoral dissertation, University of Michigan.

Quinn, R. W. (2005). Flow in knowledge work: High performance experience in the design of national security technology. *Administrative Science Quarterly, 50*(4), 610–641.

Rathunde, K., & Csíkszentmihályi, M. (2006). The development of the person: An experiential perspective. In W. Damon & R. M. Lerner (Eds.), *Handbook of child psychology* (Vol. 1, pp. 465–515). Hoboken, NJ: Wiley.

Rheinberg, F. (1991). Flow-experience when motorcycling: A study of a special human condition. In R. Brendicke (Ed.), *Safety, environment, future. Proceedings of the 1991 international motorcycle conference* (forschungsheft nr 7) (pp. 349–362). Bochum: Institut für Zweiradsicherheit (ifZ).

Russell, W. (2001). An examination of flow state occurrence in college athletes. *Journal of Sport Behaviour, 24*(1), 83–107.

Salanova, M., Bakker, A. B., & Llorens, S. (2006). Flow at work: Evidence for an upward spiral of personal and organizational resources. *Journal of Happiness Studies, 7*(1), 1–22.

Salanova, M., Rodríguez-Sánchez, A. M., Schaufeli, W. B., & Cifre, E. (2014). Flowing together: A longitudinal study of collective efficacy and collective flow among workgroups. *The Journal of Psychology, 148*(4), 435–455.

Sato, I. (1988). Bosozoku: Flow in Japanese motorcycle gangs. In M. Csíkszentmihályi & I. Csíkszentmihályi (Eds.), *Optimal experience: Psychological studies of flow in consciousness* (pp. 92–117). Cambridge: Cambridge University Press.

Sawyer, R. K. (2003). *Group creativity: Music, theater, collaboration*. Mahwah, NJ: Lawrence Erlbaum Associates.

Sawyer, R. K. (2006). Group creativity: Musical performance and collaboration. *Psychology of Music, 34*(2), 148–165.

Sawyer, R. K. (2007). *Group genius: The creative power of collaboration*. New York: Basic Books.

Schüler, J. (2012). The dark side of the moon. In S. Engeser (Ed.), *Advances in flow research* (pp. 123–137). New York, NY: Springer.

Schüler, J., & Pfenninger, M. (2011). Flow impairs risk perception in kayakers. In B. D. Geranto (Ed.), *Sport Psychology* (pp. 237–246). New York, NY: Nova Publishers.

Snow, K. Y. (2010). Work relationships that flow: Examining the interpersonal flow experience, knowledge sharing, and organizational commitment. Doctoral Dissertation, Claremont Graduate University. Retrieved from http://gradworks.umi.com/34/36/3436590.html.

Tse, D. C. K., Lau, V. W.-Y., Perlman, R., & McLaughlin, M. (2018). The development and validation of the autotelic personality questionnaire. *Journal of Personality Assessment*. https://doi.org/10.1080/00223891.2018.1491855.

Ullén, F., de Manzano, Ö., Almeida, R., Magnusson, P. K. E., Pedersen, N. L., Nakamura, J., et al. (2012). Proneness for psychological flow in everyday life: Associations with personality and intelligence. *Personality and Individual Differences, 52*(2), 167–172.

Van den Hout, J. J. J. (2016). *Team flow: From concept to application.* Dissertation, Eindhoven University of Technology, Eindhoven.

Van Schaik, P., Martin, S., & Vallance, M. (2012). Measuring flow experience in an immersive virtual environment for collaborative learning. *Journal of Computer Assisted Learning, 28*(4), 350–365.

Walker, C. J. (2010). Experiencing flow: Is doing it together better than doing it alone? *The Journal of Positive Psychology, 5*(1), 3–11.

Zimbardo, P. G. (1969). The human choice: Individuation, reason, and order versus deindividuation, impulse and chaos. In W. J. Arnold & D. Levine (Eds.), *Nebraska symposium on motivation* (pp. 237–307). Lincoln: University of Nebraska Press.

Zumeta, L., Basabe, N., Wlodarzyk, A., Bobowik, M., & Paez, D. (2016). Shared flow and positive collective gatherings. *Anales de Psicologia, 32*(3), 717–727. https://doi.org/10.6018/analesps.32.3.261651.

Chapter 3
Team Flow Theory—A Multi-level Perspective

Based on the extensive literature in Chapter 2, this explores the conceptualization of the team flow model designed by Van den Hout (2016) in depth. It shows how individual and team flow are interrelated and describes the elements that comprise a team flow experience. It goes on to show how team flow emerges and what the benefits are of experiencing team flow. Finally, it gives an indication of what the possibilities of applying team flow in a business context might be.

3.1 Defining Teams

If the individual has the opportunity to experience flow in any facet of daily life, then it stands to reason that multiple individuals can be in flow at the same time, even when they are involved in the same cooperative activity. The challenge, however, is that when multiple people are involved one also needs to consider the dynamics among the members of the group, which adds new dimensions to flow when it is experienced at the team level.

Before diving deeply into the complex workings of flow and interpersonal dynamics, it is important to clarify exactly what we mean by a team. We use Katzenbach and Smith's (1993) definition of a team: "a small number of people with complementary skills who are committed to a common purpose, set of performance goals, and approach for which they hold themselves mutually accountable" (p. 112). Most of the academic research on teams uses a definition similar to this one, and for several reasons. First, it is hard to conceive of a large number of people being part of the same cooperative dynamic—at a certain size (never precisely determined by research), groups tend to break into subgroups with their own separate dynamics. Second, the requirement of complementary skills emphasizes the fact that it is a task that one person cannot do alone. There is an important difference between taking a big job and dividing it into five parallel tasks that require the same skill (say, having 8 people move 40 boxes) and a big job that

Jef J. J. van den Hout and O. C. Davis, *Team Flow*, SpringerBriefs in Well-Being and Quality of Life Research, https://doi.org/10.1007/978-3-030-27871-7_3

requires multiple skills to do (e.g., creating an illustrated book). Working in parallel does not call for a team dynamic in which there is interplay among the participants, whereas combining disparate skill sets to create an integrated product demands that people work together effectively. Thus, skill complementarity naturally reflects the concepts of common purpose and mutual accountability, particularly because the failure of any single member of the team to finish their part of the task causes the entire team to fail to achieve the common goal. As such, accountability also facilitates the team dynamic in that it creates a forum for feedback and interaction, which in turn keeps the team cohesive and guides how each member of the team applies their unique skillset.

We should also provide some conception of what we mean by the term *team dynamic*. We use Forsyth's (2009) definition of a team dynamic being the sum of all of the actions, processes, and changes that happen within a team, either holistically or among its members. This collection of forces affects the team's behavior and performance and is created by any number of factors. The nature of the project, for example, can determine whether people work more as individuals or in smaller (sub)teams, how often tasks need to be handed off, and how frequent and detailed task feedback needs to be. The personalities within the team and the working relationships between its members can likewise play a major role in the team dynamic, such as when two people have been working together for many years while everyone else is new to the team, or when you have a couple of introverts on an otherwise extraverted team. The environment also affects team dynamics; working in tight spaces or under noisy conditions naturally affects mood and communication. For all of these forces and others, there are both constructive and destructive possibilities that affect the team's dynamic not by what they are, but by how they are applied. A small space, for example, can make it easier for everyone to focus simultaneously on specific aspects of the project, but it can also make it easier for people to get on each other's nerves. Similarly, a duo that has been working together for a long time could end up isolating itself and detracting from the dynamic, or they can use the trust and psychological safety they have established with each other as a foundation the team to build on.

3.2 Flow in Business Teams

In recent years, employees have increasingly organized themselves into groupings, such as project teams, task forces, self-managing teams and working groups (Carton & Cummings, 2012; Guzzo & Dickson, 1996). They do so in order to improve their collective performance. Teaming up is a way for people to join forces and act more swiftly and decisively (Katzenbach & Smith, 1993). This is what the current market demands. For organizations to continue to exist, they must deliver high quality against low costs, often under a tight deadline. As a consequence, employees find themselves in high-pressure environments, subjected to a lot of stress and its many undesirable effects on performance and well-being.

If the work environment were organized in a way that allows employees to experience flow as they tackle shared challenges, it would most likely result in increased enjoyment, satisfaction, personal development and shared performance. People will perform better together and their experience with team flow will likely encourage them to tackle new and even greater shared challenges. Such phenomenal results make it worthwhile to investigate whether there really is such a thing as team flow and whether the social system needed to enable team flow can be realized in the modern workplace.

The reason team flow is introduced as a new construct is the rising importance of the team in organizations. In today's economy, companies face a challenging business environment in which tasks must be performed that are so complex that teams are required to accomplish key objectives. Moreover, the complexity of these tasks often requires that individuals with different knowledge, skills, and expertise work together to accomplish them. In response, many large companies have transformed from hierarchical organizations to organizations defined by purpose, process, and people (Ghoshal & Bartlett, 1999). This has resulted in middle management perspectives becoming the subject of study, which includes the examination of management roles (Bartlett & Ghoshal, 1997), delegation (Dobrajska, Billinger, & Karim, 2015), leadership styles (Beatty & Lee, 1992), and management actions (Mantere, 2008). In this new development, teams play an important role, making the improvement of team performance an important subject of study. The literature on teams has notably explored what makes teams effective in terms of efficiency, productivity, response times, quality, customer satisfaction and innovation (Cohen & Bailey, 1997). For instance, when managers share similar mental models of task processes and outcomes, they are more likely to understand one another's perspectives, communicate more easily, coordinate more effectively, and improve overall team performance (Salas & Cannon-Bowers, 2001; Wooldridge, Schmid, & Floyd, 2008). Further potential advantages to using teams instead of individuals include synergistic levels of performance and creativity, increased flexibility and reductions in production costs and absenteeism (Delarue, Van Hootegem, Procter & Burridge, 2008; Larson, 2010; Richter, Dawson & West, 2011).

Unfortunately, teams are also associated with problems of coordination, motivation, trust, conflict, status and ego (Hackman, 1998; Lencioni, 2002; Steiner, 1972). Although the value of cohesive, high-performing teams is obvious, creating them can be something of a challenge, especially in the context of ad hoc business teams. One of the keys to accomplishing this is focusing not just on building a healthy team dynamic, but also on intrinsic motivation, satisfaction, and psychological well-being at the individual and team levels (Hackman & Wageman, 2005). Indeed, past research has shown a number of connections between these concepts and creativity, productivity, and company performance (Dolan & Metcalfe, 2012; Fisher, 2010; Lyubomirsky, King, & Diener, 2005; Wright & Cropanzano, 2004). Companies ought therefore focus on intrinsic motivation, satisfaction, and psychological well-being at the individual, team, and even organizational levels (Fisher, 2010). To give just one example, research has shown that positive mood correlates to perceived degrees of skill, interest, and self-motivation in achievement-oriented employees, all of which contribute to higher performance (Eisenberger, Jones, Stinglhamber, Shanock, & Randall, 2005).

Katzenbach and Smith (1993) define a team as "*a small number of people with complementary skills who are committed to a common purpose, set of performance goals, and approach for which they hold themselves mutually accountable*" (p. 112). There are any number of other definitions of and perspectives on the team across the literature. Most of them describe a team as a special kind of group with a well-developed collective identity that works as a unit to achieve a specific goal or set of goals, which in turn makes the team members interdependent to a significant degree.

Weggeman, Lammers and Akkermans (2007) introduce the term *collective flow* as an extension of Csíkszentmihályi's flow. Collective flow applies to situations in which many workers experience high-level process aesthetics while working together on the same artefact at the same time and in the same process. According to Weggeman et al. (2007), the experience of high-level process aesthetics is the experience of beauty people have when participating in the creation of an artefact. This can happen in any creation experience, be it playing the violin in a symphony orchestra, repairing a machine, or preparing a meal. This description of collective flow is congruent with Csíkszentmihályi's study of surgeons, where one of the surgeons explained the flow experience like this:

> It's very satisfying and if it is somewhat difficult it is also exciting. It's very nice to make things work again, to put things in their right place so that they look as they should and fit neatly. This is very pleasant, particularly when the group works together in a smooth and efficient manner: then the *aesthetics* [emphasis added] of the whole situation can be appreciated (Csíkszentmihályi, 1975, p. 129).

Weggeman et al. (2007) assume that the whole point of experiencing 'process aesthetics' is that beautiful processes often lead to good results. The ability to produce beauty in the process, the outcome, or both motivates people to start projects and to stick with them. How often members of an organization have aesthetically pleasing work experiences (flow) therefore determines, at least in part, how engaged they are. This leads Weggeman et al. (2007) to the proposition that organizations should be designed to foster flow experiences at both the individual and collective levels.

3.3 Team Flow Definition

Applying these definitions of a team and its dynamics to a flow experience, we define team flow as a shared experience of flow during the execution of interdependent personal tasks in the interest of the team, originating from an optimized team dynamic and typified by seven prerequisites and four characteristics. This conception has several key details, the first of which is the fact that the experience is shared. Each individual member of the team is experiencing flow at the same time as they pursue the team's goals. The second detail, an optimized team dynamic, reflects the optimality of the flow experience and is a complex phenomenon that requires integrating both flow and effective interpersonal interactions that are conducive to promoting and maintaining the integrity of the team. Those interactions relate to the prerequisites and characteristics of team flow, and will be discussed later on in this chapter.

Understanding team flow begins with recognizing that the individual and the team are both inextricable parts of creating the flow experience, even though neither has full control over it. The team's dynamic guides the actions of the individual, but the reverse is also true. As Csíkszentmihályi (1990, p. 65) noted:

> Surgeons say that during a difficult operation they have the sensation that the entire operating team is a single organism, moved by the same purpose; they describe it as a 'ballet' in which the *individual* [emphasis added] is subordinated to the group performance, and all involved share in a feeling of harmony and power.

That is, the team, united by its *raison(s) d'etre*, can establish one or more goals, but these same goals can be modified by individuals, and individuals can alter the aims of other individuals or even of subsets of the team. In turn, these updated goals can affect the team's goals, and so on. The team dynamic can also be altered by the internal or external feedback about the progress of some or all of the team members. The team situation is constantly in flux, as it is a complex function of individuals (singly and in subsets) and the whole team affecting each other. Thus, for each element of team flow, we will explore the construct in terms of the individual and of the team, both separately and together.

3.4 Bridging Individual Flow and Team Flow

Looking back to individual flow, establishing clear goals, feedback mechanisms, and alignment of the challenge with skills are all aspects of the flow experience that can be affected by the individual. These can be developed by promoting deep focus and a sense of control, and choosing an autotelic activity, all of which can be emergent properties of flow, but are also at least somewhat under the individual's control. The merging of action and awareness, loss of reflective self-consciousness, and time distortion remain almost entirely out of the control of the individual, and tend to be the final emergent indicators of a full-on flow experience. Notably, however, goals, feedback mechanisms, and challenge-skill balance can all evolve over the course of the flow experience, and can be affected by context and/or the other six characteristics. Indeed, research has shown that flow is actually a complex (as opposed to linear) phenomenon, in which each of the factors, both separately and in any combination, can affect any other individual factor or combination thereof. Thus, while there is an intuitive way to group the characteristics of flow, which we do here so we can focus on the prerequisites of flow, we recommend that you keep an open mind as to how the characteristics of flow can interact. After all, sometimes things don't go the way people plan, and it really is possible to foster team flow starting at any point.

In summary, the recommended starting point for team flow experiences is the presence of a collective ambition, which readily guides the process of putting in place the prerequisites for team flow. In turn, they can activate a team flow experience in which the individual is subordinated to the team's performance, and all involved share in feelings of unity, joint progress, mutual trust and holistic focus. These specific aspects of the team flow experience distinguish the team flow experience from the individual task flow experience. The experience of team flow is meaningful and satisfying to the individual team members in a way that solitary flow experiences can't be. Other attendant benefits of team flow experiences include the desire to reconvene as a team, enhancement of the team's effectiveness, and increased creativity and performance among the team members.

Figure 3.1 is a representation of all the prerequisites and characteristics of both team and individual flow. It is important to note that all of them are connected, but we've only marked some connections with arrows. The connectors between elements of individual task flow mark which elements can serve as prerequisites *or* characteristics as context demands (which is also why there are 12 boxes for individual task flow rather than 9). The double-ended arrows mark which team-level elements were derived from elements of individual task flow. The single-ended arrows indicate causal links and form a useful reminder of how team flow is created and where to intervene when it is absent. The Team Flow Model can help with that as well. In fact, we recommend that you use the Team Flow Model as a tool for reflection as you work with teams to create or maintain an environment conducive to team flow.

Figure 3.1, then, puts the prerequisites for team flow, the prerequisites for individual task flow, the characteristics of individual task flow and the

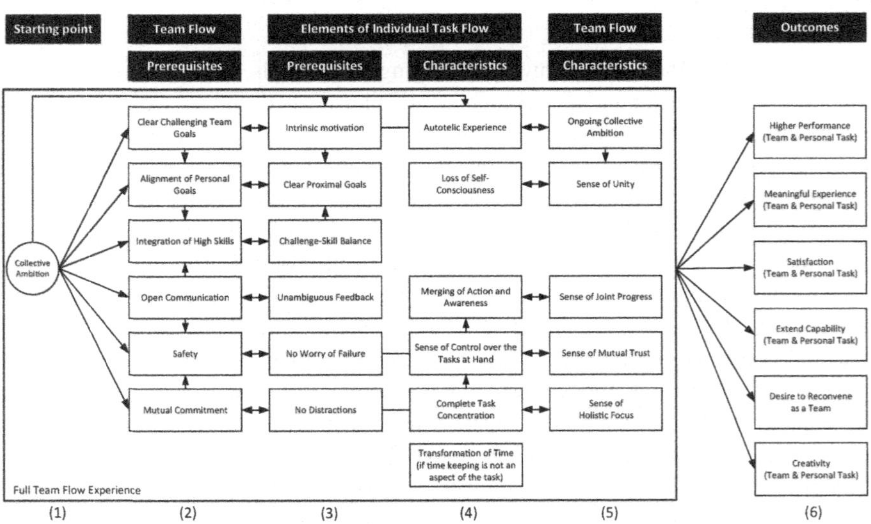

Fig. 3.1 The elements of individual task flow, team flow and their outcomes

characteristics of team flow side by side. The prerequisites for team flow (column 2) foster the prerequisites for individual flow (column 3). The prerequisites for individual flow, in turn, allow the individual to experience the characteristics of individual task flow (column 4). When all team members experience the characteristics for flow indirectly due to the prerequisites for team flow, the additional characteristics for team flow can be experienced (column 5). Moments of team flow most readily originate with a collective ambition that ties the team together and culminate in a host of positive outcomes for the team (column 6). When all the elements are overtly evident, a full team flow experience is happening.

3.5 The Prerequisites of Team Flow

The first elements of team flow that need to be considered are the ones that establish a foundation both of solid team dynamics and of a context and/or structure for the team's activities that will be conducive to flow at both the team and individual levels. These *prerequisites* of team flow can be established by the team and/or its members, and set the stage for the emergence of a flow experience.

As with individual flow, it is a good idea to start with a clear goal. This immediately presents a complication for teams. since flow requires that the goal be in line with a person's intrinsic motivation. But at the team level there is no *de facto* establishment of such motivation, and thus no activity that is autotelic *per se*. Thus, we recommend that the team begin by establishing a *collective ambition*. This *raison d'etre* of the team is shaped by the *whys* that underlie the team's formation, the values and beliefs that the team and its members maintain about how one should accomplish goals (both in general, and in relation to any goals chosen by this team), and their knowledge of each other, particularly in terms of skill sets.

3.5.1 Collective Ambition

The collective ambition is the nucleus around which the team forms and to which everyone feels connected. The first time a team is established, it is often the team's purpose and dynamic that will enable members to find autotelic activities, and in turn this can aggregate to a group-level experience of autotelicity as individuals pursue the team's shared goal. Although it would appear from this that the autotelic aspect of team flow is emergent, and indeed it is, the collective ambition remains directly dependent upon the concrete shared goal(s) of the team and the [intrinsic] reasons people choose to involve themselves with the team. As people's reasons for joining and working in a team, along with the specific tasks to accomplish, are largely, if not entirely, controlled by the people involved, the bases for collective ambition are not emergent. Still, even though a team's identity can coalesce around tasks and choices, it is only when the pursuit of the concrete aims becomes *autotelic* (i.e., that the process matters more than the result) that the team has established a collective ambition and will want to reconvene for further tasks. Thankfully, collective ambition is recursive, and a team that has established this can access and evolve it repeatedly as the team takes on new tasks. As such, we cite collective ambition as the first foundation, because it can ultimately facilitate and/or underlie effective establishment of the other prerequisites and characteristics of team flow (Van den Hout, 2016).

The difference between a collective ambition and a goal may seem subtle, but it reveals an important part of team building. For instance, suppose that a design firm establishes a project team because of a client's need. The team's goal becomes completing the task that the client requested, but that is *not* the reason the team was formed. Rather, the instantiation of the team stems from the fact that no single individual can accomplish the goal alone. As such, the team must have been built because a combination of skill sets, experiences, and personalities was needed to create the requisite synergy for accomplishing the goal. Understanding the reasoning behind the team's construction reveals the *raison d'etre* that is so fundamental to the opportunity to create team flow, and thus the team should take the time to examine how, and *why*, it came into being. In this, the team develops a collective ambition to integrate its various personalities, abilities, perspectives, etc. into an entity that has the wherewithal to accomplish goals like the one requested by the client. From there, the team is capable of applying its collective ambition to a specific goal. A collective ambition is thus about becoming the kind of team that has a set of capabilities, like a rowing squad that strives for excellence expressed through smooth, powerful, and quick rowing. The team's goal, however, is more concrete, such as medaling at the Olympics.

3.5.2 Common Goal

A team's *common goal* should be concrete, and clear to every member of the team, such that each individual understands how to contribute. Properly, a common goal should be something ambitious and challenging, clear to all members of the team, and internalized by all of the members of the team, or clear, challenging, and collective (CCC) for short. Each of these aspects is important and sets the foundation for other aspects of team flow. A clear goal helps team members understand what they need to do and facilitates honest feedback and accountability. A challenging goal creates meaning and inspires everyone to apply their skills to the fullest (high skill integration). A collective goal can be internalized by the team members so they can start aligning their personal goals with the team's.

3.5.3 Aligned Personal Goals

The *alignment of personal goals with the team's* is when the common goal gels with the personal goals of each member of the team, and has been internalized by each team member. We often advise teams to go around and make sure that there is a clear and meaningful benefit for every member of the team, and that there are no conflicts between anyone's personal goals and those of the team. This process allows people to generate a clear link between their unique skills/experiences and meeting the team's goals. Afterwards, it is helpful to discuss how the team will coordinate the efforts of its members, assign/define tasks, and develop efficient procedures. Such a process also facilitates ownership of the goals at both the individual and team levels because everyone gets a say in what is to be done, how it is to be done, and who will do it.

3.5.4 High Skill Integration

Just as individual flow requires comparable levels of challenge and skill, so too does the team need *high skill integration*. The idea is to distribute the tasks in light of the available skills and the levels at which people have them in order to provide each team member with a commensurate challenge. A key piece of the puzzle, however, is remembering that the task is not being performed by the individual in a vacuum, but rather in concert with the efforts of other team members that are all directed towards a common, internalized goal. It is thus important to remember that part of the challenge for each individual is coordinating efforts. That also allows for team members helping each other to find the optimum level of challenge. In some cases, a given subtask may not hold enough challenge, but the assignment of a second task can increase the difficulty by necessitating multitasking and/or speed.

3.5.5 Open Communication

Integral to facilitating high skill integration, as well as many key aspects of the team dynamic, is *open communication*. Parallel to the clear-and-timely-feedback characteristic of individual flow, the team needs to communicate at multiple levels to ensure the progress of individuals, sub-teams, and the team at large. As the team's deliverables coalesce, everyone needs to know how contributions are developing and accordingly make real-time adjustments to their efforts. This involves identifying errors, giving and receiving constructive feedback, offering advice, and asking questions, all of which likewise contribute to team members' situational awareness and ability to respond in accordance with the team's goals and dynamics. In the process, feedback is occurring at multiple levels. Individuals progress according to their own judgment, but also take in what they see of others' progress and the information that team members (singly and jointly) are providing. Concurrently, the team develops a degree of interdependence as they hold themselves and each other mutually accountable for the results. Notably, this only happens when all members of the team adopt the team's goals as their own.

Through open communication, the team is able to develop not just lines of feedback and accountability, but a shared mental model of the entire field of activities that the team is pursuing in order to accomplish the goal. This includes jargon, abbreviations, and even tacit ways of communicating that not only speed up the process, but also help team members identify with the group that uses these unique communications. In order to get to this point, however, every member of the team needs to perceive the others as active and perceptive listeners who attend to the verbal and non-verbal information presented. Likewise, everyone needs to maintain positivity, such that both speaking and listening are positive, non-judgmental (except when necessary), and accepting, all of which contributes not only to open communication, but to psychological safety.

3.5.6 Safety

In 2016, Google published the findings of its internal studies on what made their teams successful (cf. Duhigg, 2016). Consistent with several decades' worth of team research, Google found that one of the most important factors to team success is psychological safety [consistent with established research by many, including Edmondson (1999)]. Looking specifically at team flow, however, we found that a broader view of *safety* is a helpful perspective. As a parallel to the individual flow construct of having no fear of failure, safety is partly about the environment in which one performs. Failure must be a real possibility, and indeed highly challenging tasks are not always completed successfully, but a safe place where failure is not feared requires an environment and resources that allow team members to take appropriate risks, learn from their mistakes, and not face unnecessary or unacceptable dangers (such as undue pressure from senior management or unrealistic timelines).

Constructive, non-judgmental communication and feedback also facilitate safety, and this is directly related to the concept of "psychological safety" (cf. Edmondson, 1999). With this degree of positivity in the feedback, team members do not fear ridicule and/or punishment for their failures. Instead, they know that they their mistakes will be met with encouragement to do better, which can allow them to reflect upon their actions and goals and make the requisite adjustments for the future (as opposed to trying to mitigate the effects of mistakes).

For instance, when the second author was consulting for a dance troupe, he found that the verbal feedback was getting too analytical and too critical. As an exercise, he had the troupe practice using only non-verbal feedback, and the entire tenor of the practice changed immediately. Without words to editorialize the feedback, all they could do was signal a partner to stop and then focus on a particular movement. Team members were demonstrating to one another, moving each other, and the sole focus was about developing the moves and coordinating them with the performance goals. Everyone felt a lot more comfortable, and the team also developed new modes of communication and feedback. A key element of the exercise was that there was no need to focus on what was wrong—after all, it is really hard to explain why a dance move is wrong without using words. Instead, the focus was on aspects that the individual can control and on the implicit confidence that the dancers have in every member's ability to get the right moves into the routine. This combination of post-error growth, confidence in one another, and non-judgmental feedback created a safe space in which team members could take effective risks and perform at the peak of their respective abilities.

3.5.7 Mutual Commitment

Effective, open communication and psychological safety both necessitate a level of mutual awareness of the team's members, and likewise a level of focus upon the individual, the individual's interactions with the team, the individual's task(s) at hand, and the tasks and outputs of other team members. To accomplish this, one must translate from the individual flow characteristic of distractions being excluded from consciousness to the team flow prerequisite of *mutual commitment*. Certainly, the individual should remove distractions where possible and devote their full attention to the tasks they were assigned, but team members can also help each other focus. This is accomplished not only through feedback, but through the interplay of communication and contributing cooperatively to one another's processes. Such coordination is dependent upon all of the team members being aware of one another's activities and how each and all of them are contributing to the collective goal.

One of the places where mutual commitment is most visible is on the volleyball court. A key part of playing volleyball is the realization that each member of the team contributes to the play regardless of whether any given person contacts the ball. Many coaches, from the first day of practice, drill into the team that, if the ball hits the floor, the entire team is at fault rather than a single individual. At the lowest levels of the sport, there is inevitably some green rookie who asks why this is so when said rookie didn't touch the ball on the play. The answer is that every player moves on the court in response to the changes in teammates' positions. That is, if one player moves, *every player* moves (watch any pro team and you will see this). The movements are guided not only by communication (such as "calling the ball"), but also by a tacit awareness of where each player is and how each person is contributing to the play. This could be anything from being in position to return a block, running a fake attack, or covering the court so that opponents cannot spike into an easily-reached part of the court.

This analogy applies universally. Each member of an effective team must be cognizant of where everyone else is, what everyone else is doing, and how their actions are moving the team. Such mutual awareness aggregates to a shared representation of how the team is organizing and executing upon the mission. This not only promotes focus, but also highlights and emphasizes the commitment to contributing to the shared goal of the team and the need to align oneself with the team's *raison d'etre*.

3.6 The Characteristics of Team Flow

Establishing the prerequisites for team flow is very much like preparing soil for planting. You are maximizing the opportunity to cultivate the very best performance from the ground and, nurtured properly, the results that emerge can be fantastic. With the seven baseline prerequisites in place, the team is in position to benefit from the four emergent characteristics of team flow that solidify the team's dynamic and create the synergy that enables peak performance.

3.6.1 Sense of Unity

The first of these four characteristics is a *sense of unity*. Building on the collective ambition of the team, members can become so immersed in the dynamic of the team that they can temporarily lose track of themselves as actors and meld into a unified team with a single identity. Similar to the individual flow construct of losing reflective self-consciousness, every team member becomes focused so completely upon the tasks and the team interactions as to stop thinking about oneself. Through the alignment of personal and team goals, one's own identity and needs become enfolded in the pursuit of the team's aims and the individual's contributions to them. The result is a seamless blend of efforts, identities, and capabilities woven into a cohesive tapestry of talents.

The most obvious example of such integration is a symphony orchestra. The string section, for instance, comprises multiple violins that play either on the same notes or in cohesive harmonies, and the redundancy creates a powerful, synergistic chorus that is far more sonorous than the results of a single player. In such moments, it becomes nearly impossible for all but the most expert to identify a single violin, and a violinist experiencing team flow feels unified with the string section in the production of this measure of music.

3.6.2 Sense of Joint Progress

One of the most striking characteristics of flow experiences is the merging of action and awareness. As with the loss of reflexive self-consciousness, one's focus becomes fixated upon the pursuit of the goals and the tasks and activities one must perform in that pursuit. There are no emails to answer, calls to return, people to attend to, or other deadlines; there is only going for the goal. At the team level, attention is narrowed to the scope of participating in, and contributing to, the team's activities, reflecting the group's unity of purpose and action. One loses track of single actors, extraneous demands, and thoughts about anything besides contributing to the flow of the team's pursuit. Every action, every thought pertains to the activities and dynamics related to achieving that which the team set out to accomplish. The resulting internal synchrony is a *sense of joint progress*: a feeling that everyone is moving forward together. A sense of making joint progress comes from coordinated actions that are experienced as effortless cooperation. It is like the team's collective awareness merges with their coordinated joint actions, delivering uplifting, elevating and gratifying experiences.

Such a sense provides ongoing feedback about the team's performance, as well as providing an indicator of what any given person should be doing. As such, team members are able to respond instantaneously to developing situations, and we see in team flow that everyone is so in tune as to react automatically and harmoniously without being aware of any thought process guiding them. Of special note is the way in which team members are able to build upon each other's work seamlessly and efficiently, such that each contribution seems almost expected. Throughout the process, the sense of joint progress gives the team a constant feeling of accomplishment and satisfaction, which seems to explode like a firework when the goal is met. One sees this frequently in teams of emergency responders as they bravely go into danger trusting each other with their lives. They have drilled, communicated, and learned each other's rhythms so completely that they can move in coordination without being able to see one another, and shift gears and tasks seamlessly as the situation progresses. To watch a solid rescue operation, for instance, is to see feats that look almost like mind-reading or telepathy as the team immediately knows what to do, even when something unexpected arises.

3.6.3 Mutual Trust

Given the interdependence of team members in pursuit of the common goal, there has to be a very deep level of *mutual trust*. The team, at both the individual and group levels, needs to know that everyone is going to perform at their best, pursue the common goal, take smart risks, provide effective feedback, et cetera. But, this also requires the recognition that one is not in control of every factor. Unlike individual flow, where the sense of control gives one a feeling of being able to address whatever comes, in team flow there has to be trust that the team can handle any situation that might arise. There is an incredible vulnerability in this trust, a willingness to depend upon others without worrying about failure and feeling fully empowered as an individual to do what it takes for the team to succeed (knowing that the others will do the same). Without the prerequisites for team flow in place, this trust can feel very risky, given that the stakes (career, income, team/company success, many long hours of work) are so high and that the team will be collectively responsible for the outcome. But in a psychologically safe environment where people are supporting each other, providing constructive feedback, sharing resources, and resolving conflict respectfully, team members promote each other's self-efficacy, which in turn aggregates to the team level as mutual trust and a feeling of team potency.

Read up on any elite military unit, and you will find this level of mutual trust being built brick by brick through the training process. Whenever a team member struggles, the others jump into help with encouragement, resources, or whatever they can provide. This slowly becomes habit, and the soldiers begin to depend upon the fact that their team is with them. Training deliberately places soldiers in difficult challenges that are insurmountable for an individual and seemingly impossible for most teams, which helps build the interdependent team mentality that sees them to the finish line when others would throw in the towel.

3.6.4 Holistic Focus

Time is a fickle thing, and rarely more so than in a flow experience. The distorted sense of time that occurs during flow can be either dilation (slowing down) or constriction (speeding up). It is not just the old adage "time flies when you're having fun," but the fact that the deep focus upon the activity can cause time to slip out of proportion. Applied to teams, we find that the entire team loses its sense of time. Everyone is so caught up in the dynamics, contributions, coordination, cooperation, sub-goals, exchanges, and so on, that no one is really sure how time is elapsing. The conception of time passing becomes relegated to events as people mark the completion of tasks, handoffs, and interactions. Ironically, there is also a very strong sense of the present, the *now*, because that is the moment in which one is operating. As action and awareness merge, seconds and minutes pass unmarked, always simply part of the now. This *now* includes everything that the individual is doing, everything the teammates are doing, and the dynamic integration of all that is occurring. As the entire team begins, individually and collectively at the same time, to experience this *holistic focus*, the team feels a total concentration upon the communally aligned field of work that has no room for timekeeping.

In Table 3.1 we summarzie all eleven elements of team flow and relate them to the nine elements of individual flow.

Table 3.1 The elements of team flow

Element	Underlying constructs	Relates to individual flow element
Prerequisites		
Collective ambition		
The extent to which the same ambition is collectively shared	Participate in the activity for its own sake; (Re)convene with the team to tackle a future challenge	Intrinsic motivation
Common goal		
A collective goal that is endorsed by everyone	Clear and meaningful to all members of the team; Compatible with members' individual goal(s); Internalized by all team members	Clear proximal goal(s)

(continued)

Table 3.1 (continued)

Element	Underlying constructs	Relates to individual flow element
Aligned personal goals		
The presence of personal goals that also contribute to the common goal	Derive from, are consistent with, and contribute to a clear and shared team goal	Clear proximal goal(s)
High skill integration		
The arrangement of individual merits into a collective strength	Knowing each other's strengths, interests, and skills; Team-level goals that require members to use their complementary skills at high levels; Facilitating the challenge-level to skill-level balance for each team member; Coordinated action	Challenges matched to skill level
Open communication		
Openness in communication with one another	Clear and unambiguous; Timely and consistent; Arises out of mutual accountability; Connects individuals' contributions to the common goal; Uses close listening; Is genuinely constructive and appropriate	Clear and immediate feedback
Safety		
The level of psychological safety needed to engage in action	Provides for potential success *and* failure; Allows for taking necessary risks; Facilitates a feeling of being safe to act; Promotes mutual respect; Fosters trust; Allows for learning and growth	No fear of failure, sense of control
Mutual commitment		
The level of commitment to one another	Full attention at the individual level; Awareness of the common goal and each other's contributions to it; No dealing with distractions external to the team's common task; Keeping one another on task; Cognizance of the interplay that is the team dynamic; Alignment with the *raison[s] d'être* and purposes of the team	Total concentration, oblivious to distraction
Characteristics		
Sense of unity		
The extent to which the team acts in unity	Cohesion; Not feeling self-conscious around other members of the team; Blending of egos	Loss of reflective self-consciousness
Sense of joint progress		
A collective feeling of accomplishment	Synergistic interactions; All activities are focused on pursuing the collective goal; Moving it forward; Creating a comprehensive feeling of accomplishment, satisfaction and elevation	Merging of action and awareness

(continued)

Table 3.1 (continued)

Element	Underlying constructs	Relates to individual flow element
Mutual trust		
The level of mutual trust in the cooperation	Willingness to be vulnerable; Mutual respect; Confidence within the task environment; Team potency/efficacy	No fear of failure, sense of control
Holistic focus		
The extent to which everyone focuses on the common goal	All team members concentrate on the task at hand; Complete alignment of each of those tasks to the common goal; Complete focus of the team as a whole on its common goal	Distorted experience of time passing, complete concentration

3.7 An Integrative Multilevel Model of Individual Task Flow and Team Flow

This chapter describes how team flow and individual task flow are related using their prerequisites and characteristics. An important difference between individual flow and team flow is that individual experiences of flow arise from a set of circumstances created, maintained, and eventually terminated by the individual. In team flow, by contrast, the individual takes part in a dynamic environment over which each member has limited control and which also limits the individual's control over the situation and circumstances in which the members (and the team) work. This team dynamic can have profound effects on both the individual and the team. For this reason, we concur with Walker (2010) and Snow (2010) when they question the notion that flow must be entirely in the control of the individual. In addition, while all flow research has made the construct contingent upon a flow activity, Van den Hout (2016) examined a flow experience that occurs because of a team dynamic that is concentrated around a common activity. In line with Kozlowski and Klein's (2000) multilevel approach, as well as Gully, Incalcaterra, Joshi and Matthew (2002) contention that constructs experienced at the individual level can be aggregated when they are being evaluated at the team level, we maintain that when a team's members are experiencing flow while pursuing the team's common purpose, there is a collective flow experience that we call team flow. Multiple research teams, including Csíkszentmihályi (1990) and Marotto, Roos and Victor (2007), concur with this view of team flow as an individual phenomenon aggregated at the team level. When analyzing flow at the team level, the elements of individual flow must be reconceptualized, since they operate differently in a team context. Given that those elements can be created by each participant during any given activity (Csíkszentmihályi, 1993), extending that idea to the team level suggests that each participant can create the elements of individual flow both for themselves and for the other members of the team. As such, these elements become embedded in the team such that each member can derive a flow experience from the team dynamic brought forth by these elements. This enables the individual flow experience to aggregate into a Gestalten team-level experience, which is to say that the team-level experience

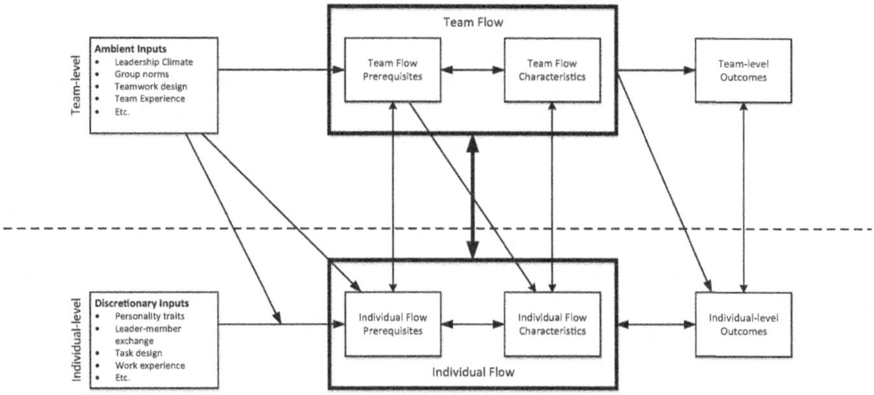

Fig. 3.2 Integrative multilevel model of individual task flow and team flow

is more intense than the sum of the individual flow experiences from which it emerges. For example, team members can set goals together, receive and give feedback on one another's progress, decide how difficult tasks should be (i.e., the challenge), make additional skills available, promote a safe environment to soothe any fears of failure, and/or help team members maintain focus by removing distractions and making necessary contributions to the team's progress. In each of these examples, and indeed in each element of team flow, an element of individual flow is merged with an aspect of team dynamics, which can then form a set of individual flow experiences that also comprise a team flow experience (see below). Therefore, van den Hout, Davis, and Weggeman (2018) proposed an integrative multilevel model of individual and team flow that is presented in Fig. 3.2.[1]

3.8 Evidence of the Existence and Consequences of Team Flow

Finding evidence of team flow requires an instrument to measure it, so Van den Hout (2016) designed and validated an instrument called the "Team Flow Monitor." This instrument is a questionnaire that measures all elements of the team flow experience. Using this instrument on a sample of 83 teams, with 433 questionnaires completed, he found support for a second-order, two-factor model of team flow. One factor represents the prerequisites of team flow, a set containing seven constructs (a collective ambition, common goal, aligned personal goals, high skill integration, open communication, safety, and mutual commitment), and the second factor represents

[1]To learn more about this model, consult the original article: *The conceptualization of Team Flow* (van den Hout et al., 2018).

the characteristics of team flow, accounting for the remaining four constructs (sense of unity, sense of joint progress, mutual trust, and holistic focus). We found that team flow describes a team-level experience in which all participating team members are completely involved in their common activity and are working together intuitively and synergistically towards the common goal (cf. Sawyer, 2006, 2007). We found considerable convergence between team members' experience of all of the elements of team flow as they execute their personal task for the team and their experience of team flow. This is in contrast to Sawyer's view that the group can be in flow even when the members are *not* (Sawyer, 2006, p. 159). Because Van den Hout's list of team flow elements covers all the elements of individual flow (adapted to allow for their experience in cooperation with other team members), it is fair to say that when team flow occurs, individual team members are necessarily experiencing flow in the performance of their tasks. The fact that there is a shared experience of flow in the team is what determines that team flow is taking place, and shows the construct to be more than a group of individuals merely experiencing flow together. Rather, it is individuals collectively and simultaneously experiencing two levels of flow while working in service of each other and the team's larger ambitions.

3.9 How Team Flow Relates to Other Flow Constructs

In Sect. 2.4 we gave an overview of extant research on interpersonal flow experiences and in Chap. 3 we described the team flow theory. In this paragraph we will bring back the constructs of Paragraph 2.4 and relate them to the team flow theory. We have said that to be able to speak of a team flow experience, everyone needs to experience flow while contributing to the team dynamic, but we also need to consider the research showing that the depth or intensity flow experiences might differ (Davis, 2010; Csíkszentmihályi, 1975; Nakamura & Csíkszentmihályi, 2009).

For instance, when a team member is not experiencing a deep level of flow (*microflow*), there is still high arousal and affect, along with satisfaction with the activity and the sense of having had a positive experience. But, there is not as much in the way of time distortion, autotelicity, and a balance of high levels of challenge and skill. Deep flow experiences, by contrast, are where all the nine elements of the flow experience are present to a significant degree (Davis, 2010). The team dynamic can have a significant effect on the level of flow experienced, both because contributing to the team dynamic can add to the challenge, and because the team's dynamic can foster engagement that can propel microflow towards a much deeper and rich [team] flow experience.

Building on this research, we would like to introduce the following distinct flow constructs that together contribute to the development of team flow:

Individual task flow: Flow experienced during the execution of personal tasks for the team's purpose varying from *microflow* to *deep flow*.

Interactive flow: Flow experienced during interactions with other team members while completing a task together. These interactions emerge from the team dynamic, and during these interactions team members get 'in sync' with each other. This is sometimes referred to as *interactional synchrony* or *flow synchronization* (cf. Walker, 2010; Keith et al., 2014; Magyaródi & Oláh, 2015). For interactive flow to take place, each person involved in the interaction should experience individual task flow and the interaction should *not* directly involve all team members simultaneously.

Contagious flow: Experiencing flow through contagion by other team member's individual task flow experiences while completing a task together. This means team members are affected by the flow experience of their fellows, increasing the intensity of their own flow experience as they perform their individual tasks. Contagion is the reason team flow often starts with one team member's individual flow experience igniting a teammate's, who ignites another and so on until a tipping point is reached where the remaining team members 'sync up' or 'plug in' to the flowing team dynamic (cf. Bakker, 2005; Walker, 2010).

Unit flow: The experience of flow at the unit level (one hierarchical layer higher than the individual level). This means that the unit's performance as an entity is functioning 'in flow', as when the collective awareness of all members in that performing unit are smoothly merging with their joint actions. At this moment the team is functioning at the peak of their abilities (cf. Sawyer's group flow definition, 2003; Salanova et al.'s collective flow definition, 2014). Unit flow doesn't occur unless *all* unit members are involved. Therefore this kind of experience of flow is also referred to as shared or collective flow (cf. Zumeta et al., 2016; Salanova et al., 2014). Often team members are aware that they are both experiencing flow while they are part of the same team dynamic. This awareness intensifies their flow experience in a positive feedback loop via contagion and interaction. We do realize that is not possible to be self-conscious and in flow at the same time, meaning that during a flow experience it is not possible that team members are aware of their own flow experience, but they could be aware of the flow experience of their team mates, since their teammates' contributions are related to their personal task. Also, we do believe that in between episodes of flow people realize that they are experiencing flow together, and that this awareness could strengthen their collective efficacy beliefs, and in turn the intensity of their flow experiences (cf. Zumeta et al., 2016; Salanova et al., 2014).

So, during experiences of team flow, all involved team members experience all the constructs listed above, and during full team flow all team members experience deep flow during the execution of their aligned personal tasks *as well as* the constructs listed above.

Further, we would like to emphasize that an experience of team flow occurs when the previously mentioned 11 elements of team flow are present and that we expect those 11 elements to correlate strongly with the presence of the constructs of individual flow described above. The 11 elements of team flow are conceptualized such that when these 11 elements are present at team level for all individual team members, the 9 elements of individual flow at task level are also present. Also, we would like to emphasize that, like the experience of individual task flow, a team flow experience lasts for a variable period of time and fluctuates in intensity throughout that time. Consequently, when all involved team members in an active team dynamic experience the 11 elements of team flow at a specific moment in time, we could identify that as a team flow experience that can fluctuate in intensity at the team level. Also, like moments of individual (task) flow, moments of team flow can happen on a regular basis, be it daily, weekly, monthly, or otherwise. When moments of team flow have emerged in a team collaboration, it is often the case that these moments are experienced more regularly until something happens to impede the team flow experience (Van den Hout, 2016; Van den Hout, Gevers, Davis, & Weggeman, 2017).

3.10 Putting the Pieces Together: The Emergence of Team Flow

Van den Hout's research has shown that one of the most important parts of the process for developing team flow is understanding the elements and having an idea of how to create them. Putting them together into a flow experience, however, requires some additional integration. It is important to keep in mind that, while we are recommending an effective way of building team flow based on our research, every team is different, and the personalities, contexts, and resources available may necessitate doing things in a different order or even allowing for some elements to develop over time. While any member of the team can create any of the prerequisites, a team with a leader or manager usually depends upon that individual to instantiate the creation of these elements, especially because said leader is usually the one with resources, the ability to choose the team, and the power to change the aims, tasks, incentives, and goals.

As noted, we suggest starting with a collective ambition. A team that begins by developing a collective ambition kicks off with drive. They know why they have come together, and they have a North Star for guiding their individual and collective efforts. No matter where they are in the process, they can pause to reorient themselves as often as necessary. In order to generate the requisite understanding to do so, it is important for the team to confer about the goals, and to discuss aloud to ensure that everyone understands and is on the same page. The importance of this process cannot be understated, and far too many teams get going on tasks before ensuring that everyone truly understands, *and buys into*, the team's collective goals and its reasons for being. Optimally, teams are chosen very intentionally, with serious thought given to the skill sets and personalities needed, but we know that this is not always a reality, especially in the business world. So, it becomes vital to take deliberate steps to construct an authentic team, to find out how everyone's personal and professional motivations can align with the collective goals of the team, and how everyone can fit into, and contribute to, the collective ambition. Often, this means creating differing incentives for various members of the team as people reveal their respective goals. Taking the time up front to delineate all of this is often the difference between success and failure, especially in an *ad hoc* team.

These two prerequisites (collective ambition, alignment of personal and team goals) established, the next hurdle is understanding which knowledge, skills, and talents are present in the team, and distributing tasks accordingly. Remember to consider not just who is good at which tasks, but also who *wants* to do which tasks. Just because people have certain talents or skills does not necessarily mean that they have a specific desire to use them all the time, which may also apply to the context of the team. Alternatively, some people may be looking for a challenge in order to grow (and hopefully to experience individual flow!). Make the assignment of tasks a collective effort rather than dealing out action items, especially because accepting tasks willingly increases the buy-into the individual goal and, by extension, to the team's goal.

Put together, the high skill integration, collective ambition, and alignment of goals form the foundation for team communication; this foundation underlies discussions about what the team is trying to do, what it is currently doing, how well it is doing in moving towards its goals, and what it should do next. Feedback often comes along these lines, as does accountability and eventually trust. As members of the team begin to accomplish tasks and milestones, they have opportunities to develop credibility with the team for what they do well, and likewise the team has the opportunity to gain credibility with the individual by providing effective and constructive feedback. This can be a challenge, so it is helpful to discuss how to give clear, encouraging, and constructive feedback in the team orientation/onboarding, with a view to providing *carte blanche* for any member of the team to speak up, share an idea, or take a smart risk (psychological safety). One of the best ways to do this is to discuss how errors and failure will be addressed in order to ensure that responses are supportive, non-judgmental, and promote growth and encouragement. Consistently constructive criticism greatly increases trust, and greater trust allows for more effective and spectacular risk-taking, along with a willingness to hear deeper and tougher feedback.

As the responses to people's outputs continue, collaboration progresses and the feedback loops develop properly, the team's open communication and psychological safety enable the team to build rapport and develop a rhythm and shared focus on the developing tasks and goals. Deliberate attention paid to these rhythms and shared focuses promote mutual commitment. This part is tricky, because over-analysis can lead to people experiencing an undue amount of feedback. The key is for all of the team members to cultivate awareness of their own individual contributions, how other people are using them in real time, and how others will use their contributions in the future. Making an effort to see and internalize a sense of this system at the individual level can aggregate to the prerequisite of mutual commitment on the team level.

With these prerequisites in place, the team will be in a position for the characteristics of team flow to emerge. As all of the team members experience the rhythm of the team's dynamic and express the team's collective ambition through their actions and outputs, the team experiences a sense of unity in which they are so deeply focused on how they are contributing that they temporarily lose track of their individual identities and the team moves as one. Through the open communication, including the supportive and constructive feedback, the team is able not just to feel the sense of unity, but also a sense of harmony, joint power, joint progress, and joint focus. Like a school of fish, every member can see not only their own progress and contributions, but also the progress of the entire system and team. Because they are a unit, and move as one, anyone can act without fear of failure or inappropriate judgment, which means that they are willing to take appropriate risks, offer their ideas, and be vulnerable, abandoning the illusion that they control everything they are in charge of. In this experience of mutual trust, everyone has faith that their collective actions will yield success, and they can trust their teammates to deliver and contribute in harmony with the team's system. As the synergy deepens, trust blooms, and a feeling of oneness both within and throughout the system flourishes, the collective dedication to holistic focus becomes most evident. The team, as individuals and as one, has total concentration upon the shared activities, contributions, collaborations, and progress. The current that this creates is the team flow of which everyone is a part.

The figure below gives a more systematic conceptualization of the concept of team flow as defined by Van den Hout (2016). It all starts with a collective ambition. The prerequisites 'collective ambition,' 'common goal,' and 'aligned personal goals' contribute strongly to shared experiences of unity. 'Collective ambition,' 'high skill integration,' and 'open communication' contribute strongly to a shared sense of progress. 'Collective ambition,' 'open communication,' and 'safety' contribute strongly to mutual trust. And finally, the 'collective ambition' with a 'common goal' and 'mutual commitment' contribute strongly to shared experiences of holistic focus. These sets of relationships, which between them support the four characteristics of team flow, form the basis of the team flow model (Fig. 3.3). This model will prove a valuable tool to future researchers seeking to learn more about the relationships among the various elements within and variables without.

Experiencing the four characteristics of team flow feeds back into the collective ambition, creating a positive feedback loop. Thanks to their experience with the four characteristics of team flow, the team members will feel a strong shared bond, will have made progress together and feel motivated by that, will trust each other more (which makes cooperation more pleasant and less stressful), will know what to expect from each other, and will have a good idea of what to do together next. These are all ingredients for cooking up a collective ambition to tackle a new challenge together.

We may conclude that all team flow prerequisites and characteristics are dynamically related and that the interrelations can be further explained by referring to the literature, field research, and common sense. The Team Flow Model by Van den Hout (2016) represents the strongest interrelations with arrows (Fig. 3.3). No model can hope to be more than a simplified representation of reality, however, and we are well aware that all of the elements are interrelated in reality. But, this final version of the Team Flow Model contains only the most important interrelations and their directions as a guide for teams seeking to create a team flow climate.

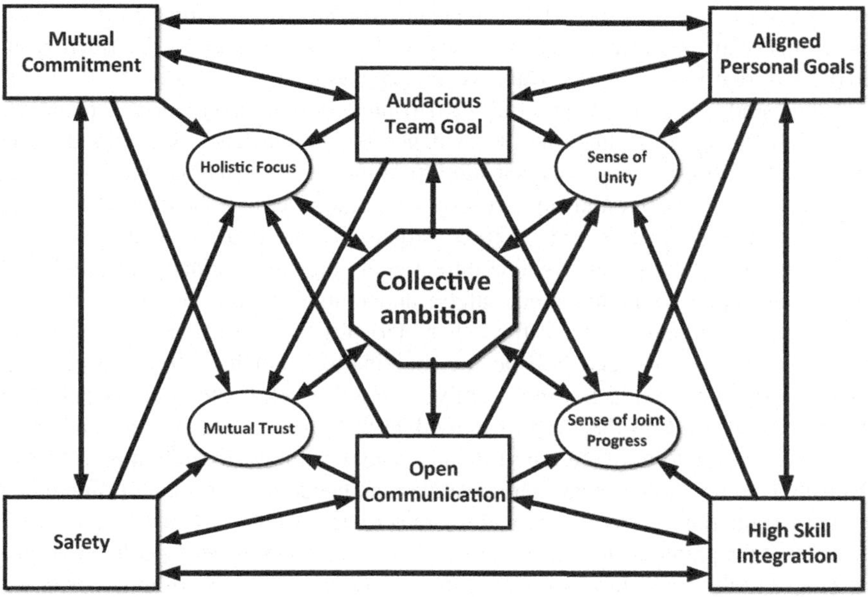

Fig. 3.3 The 11 elements of the Team Flow Model (Van den Hout, 2016). Note: 6 prerequisites (rectangles) emerge over two stages from the prerequisite of collective ambition (octagon). Once the prerequisites are established, the four characteristics of team flow (ovals) emerge, thus instantiating team flow. This, in turn, fuels collective ambition. Although all relationships are bi-directional, and all 11 elements are connected, this figure indicates only the most important relationships

3.11 The Benefits of Team Flow

Now that we understand how teams are able to experience team flow, a new question arises: "How does the experience of team flow within professional organizations affect individual- and team-level outcomes?" From the research on individual flow, we know that task-related flow involves full dedication to the task with an intense focus and full concentration, such that the performance of the task seems to be spontaneous and effortless (Csíkszentmihályi, 1990, 1996; Nakamura & Csíkszentmihályi, 2009). This optimal experience in which the subject is deeply motivated to persist in their activities will naturally lead to better performance (Landhäußer & Keller, 2012) and high satisfaction (Csíkszentmihályi, 1990, 1996, 2003). When these individual flow experiences come together in a team environment, team members reinforce each other so that the team as a whole can excel.

With this in mind, Van den Hout researched the effects of team flow in the work environment. He found positive relationships between individual flow and team flow with respect to work-related outcomes at both the individual and team level, which is in line with the research on individual flow. Team flow correlates positively with team-level outcomes like team positivity and individual-level outcomes like the percentage of time a team member experienced individual task flow and individual team members' respective levels of general happiness (Van den Hout, 2016; Van den Hout, Gevers, Davis & Weggeman,2019)

In his study, Van den Hout et al. (2019) proved the convergence of members' team flow perceptions, thus offering evidence for the existence of both individual and collective flow experiences that stem from the team's dynamic. Moreover, Van den Hout et al. (2019) found support for the second-order two-factor model of team flow, with the aforementioned seven constructs that are considered the team flow prerequisites (collective ambition, common goal, aligned personal goals, high skill integration, open communication, safety, and mutual commitment) and the four constructs comprising the team flow characteristics (sense of unity, sense of joint progress, mutual trust, and holistic focus). Finally, team flow (prerequisites and characteristics) proved to be significantly related to work-related outcomes both at the individual level, in the form of individual task flow and happiness, and at the team level, in the form of team performance and general positivity within the team. A positive team climate (with more positive than negative expressions) is predicted by both team flow prerequisites and characteristics, which is consistent with our theory that the prerequisites together foster a climate where effective collaboration is possible and the characteristics deliver the experience of a sense of unity, progress, trust, and shared focus. Van den Hout et al. (2019) has shown that team flow exists as a team-level construct and is related to a number of individual and team-level outcomes that are known to be very important for sustaining a healthy and productive work force. Generally speaking, these results show that the prerequisites for team flow are most relevant to improving team performance. For the experience of happiness, the presence of the characteristics of team flow is most relevant, as only the characteristics of team flow can deliver a truly gratifying experience.

In a follow-up study about the effects of team flow in a work environment, Verhoeven (2018) researched whether the experience of team flow would lead to more effective teams in terms of team creativity, team performance, and team satisfaction. His positive results fit in nicely with the findings of Van den Hout (2016) and further strengthen the idea that team flow is related to a number of positive team-level outcomes that are important for sustaining a healthy and productive work force.

Van den Hout (2016) shows that teams have considerable influence on the way individual employees feel about work in the sense that they experience a more positive work environment and increased happiness when the elements for team flow are present. Once the team flow kicks in, the experience of synergy, control, trust, and high performance is unparalleled. The team develops a strong bond and familiarity that fuels their collective ambition for the future, creating a positive feedback loop that makes teams more prone to experiencing team flow in the future. The benefits of team flow are many, in both the short term and the long. The effortless feeling of performing at one's best, and the high quality of the outcome, reinforce self-efficacy at both the individual and team levels, which increases the probability of future successes. Team flow also fuels motivation at all levels, which incites people to put in more effort, sometimes even discretionary effort. When commitment is high, and growth is consistent, team members are dedicated and developing, which entails increased skill levels and better performance. The emotional highs of flow experiences promote emotional and physiological well-being, and this translates to a better work environment not only for those who experience flow, but for the people around them. One of the most important results, however, is that team flow experiences almost always occur in the presence of meaningful goals, which provides an additional layer of satisfaction, commitment, engagement, and personal and professional well-being. As a result, team flow allows individuals to experience well-being in the form self-determination through experiences of autonomy and competence in their own tasks and discretionary efforts, and personal connection through their team interactions. Thus, while building team flow is effortful and time consuming, especially when a team is first convened, the benefits to the individual, the team, and the work environment are exceptionally worthwhile. Practitioners who are interested in improving the likelihood of team flow experiences and its desirable outcomes should devote time and energy to putting in place the prerequisites for team flow. Because more and more people work in teams these days, it is important to mention effects that probably go beyond the benefits of individual experiences of flow. The prophylactic value of team flow, plus the improved team performance, make it important to create the conditions for team flow within teams and keep the work environment healthy and conducive to excellence.

3.12 The Possibilities of Applying Team Flow

Flow is a helpful gauge of team functioning whose absence can signal trouble before actual problems reveal themselves. As such, it is a highly valuable tool for monitoring team dynamics or similar aspects, and can be a benchmark for figuring out what a team needs to perform at a higher or more synchronous level. We intend for our theory on team flow to provide a common language for scholars and practitioners and shed light on unanswered questions in the literature relevant to flow and work teams.

Business is changing and becoming more dynamic. With the advent of the Knowledge Era, expertise and creativity are becoming the bases of commerce, which is causing jobs and tasks to become increasingly complex and is forcing people to specialize (Rousseau, 1997). Because of this, there is greater focus on heuristic tasks (creativity) rather than algorithmic tasks (cf. Amabile, Conti, Coon, Lazenby & Herron, 1996; Hennessey & Amabile, 2010). This increased complexity also means that many tasks require multiple specialists to complete them, which necessitates the formation of a team. That is why it is so important to know how to maximize team performance, and flow is a means to creativity and high performance (Csíkszentmihályi, 1990, among others) that our research has extended to business teams.

The essence of a team is shared commitment. Without it, teams perform as clusters of individuals; with it, they become powerful units of collective performance. The best teams invest a tremendous amount of time into shaping a purpose that they can own. They also translate their purpose into specific performance goals, and members of successful teams pitch in and become accountable with and to their teammates. The fundamental distinction between teams and other forms of work groups revolves around the means for attaining high performance. A work group relies on the individual contributions of its members for group performance, but a team strives for something greater than what its members could achieve individually (Katzenbach & Smith, 1993). An effective team is always capable of more than the sum of its members' abilities. For managers, the key is to know how to build a team of people with a mission and complementary skills, and then empower them to develop the prerequisites of team flow.

Team flow could be a strong indicator that a group is flourishing, and its absence can suggest a need for intervention long before problems (e.g., low performance, low motivation) arise. As such, the presence or absence of team flow becomes a valuable diagnostic, and observing which aspects of the construct are missing can provide clues to a *set* of factors to adjust instead of having to modulate single, isolated factors to discover which of them are inhibiting performance.

Team flow puts the team into a situation where its members are all completely involved in their common activity; an experience whose synergistic nature supports the creation of more team flow in a virtuous circle. During experiences of team flow, the team is in control as a unit, reacts swiftly as a unit, and accomplishes goals as a unit. Each of the team members' actions will flow naturally from what came before and overall performance will increase with every moment the team stays in flow. Those who have experienced team flow describe it as a unique experience they wanted to perpetuate or, failing that, at least experience again.

In summary, the occurrence of team flow likely improves team performance and provides individual team members with a meaningful and satisfying experience. Team flow also fosters a desire to reconvene as a team (*autotelicity*) and represents a mastery experience that extends the team's capabilities.

References

Amabile, T. M., Conti, R., Coon, H., Lazenby, J., & Herron, M. (1996). Assessing the work environment for creativity. *Academy of Management Journal, 39*(5), 1154–1184.

Bakker, A. B. (2005). Flow among music teachers and their students: The crossover of peak experiences. *Journal of Vocational Behavior, 66*(1), 26–44.

Bartlett, C. A., & Ghoshal, S. (1997). The myth of the generic manager: New personal competencies for new management roles. *California Management Review, 40*(1), 92–116.

Beatty, C. A., & Lee, G. L. (1992). Leadership among middle managers: An exploration in the context of technological change. *Human Relations, 45*(9), 957–989.

Carton, A. M., & Cummings, J. N. (2012). A theory of subgroups in work teams. *Academy of Management Review, 37*(3), 441–470.

Cohen, S. G., & Bailey, D. E. (1997). What makes teams work: group effectiveness: Research from the shop floor to the executive suite. *Journal of Management, 23*(3), 239–290.

Csíkszentmihályi, M. (1975). *Beyond boredom and anxiety*. San Francisco, CA: Jossey-Bass Publishers.

Csíkszentmihályi, M. (1990). *Flow: The psychology of optimal experience*. New York: Harper and Row.

Csíkszentmihályi, M. (1993). *The evolving self: A psychology for the third millennium*. New York: HarperCollins.

Csíkszentmihályi, M. (1996). *Creativity: Flow and the psychology of discovery and invention*. New York: HarperCollins.

Csikszentmihalyi, M. (2003). *Good business: Leadership, flow, and the making of meaning*. New York, NY: Penguin Books.

Davis, O. C. (2010). *Defining microflow through the context of a waiting paradigm*. Dissertation: Claremont Graduate University.

Delarue, A., Van Hootegem, G., Procter, S., & Burridge, M. (2008). Teamworking and organizational performance: A review of survey-based research. *International Journal of Management Reviews, 10*(2), 127–148.

Dobrajska, M., Billinger, S., & Karim, S. (2015). Delegation within hierarchies: How information processing and knowledge characteristics influence the allocation of formal and real decision authority. *Organization Science, 26*(3), 687–704.

Dolan, P., & Metcalfe, R. (2012). The relationship between innovation and subjective wellbeing. *Research Policy, 41*(8), 1489–1498.

Duhigg, C. (2016). What Google learned from its quest to build the perfect team. *The New York Times Magazine, 26,* 2016.

Edmondson, A. (1999). Psychological safety and learning behavior in work teams. *Administrative Science Quarterly, 44*(2), 350–383.

Eisenberger, R., Jones, J. R., Stinglhamber, F., Shanock, L., & Randall, A. T. (2005). Flow experiences at work: for high need achievers alone? *Journal of Organizational Behavior, 26* (7), 755–775.

Fisher, C. D. (2010). Happiness at work. *International Journal of Management Reviews, 12*(4), 384–412.

Forsyth, D. R. (2009). *Group dynamics*. Belmont, CA: Wadsworth, Cengage Learning.

Ghoshal, S., & Bartlett, C. A. (1999). *The individualized corporation: A fundamentally new approach to management*. New York: HarperCollins.

Gully, S. M., Incalcaterra, K. A., Joshi, A., & Matthew, J. (2002). A meta-analysis of team-efficacy, potency, and performance: Interdependence and level of analysis as moderators of observed relationships. *Journal of Applied Psychology, 87*(5), 819–832.

Guzzo, R. A., & Dickson, M. W. (1996). Teams in organizations: Recent research on performance and effectiveness. *Annual Review of Psychology, 47*(1), 307–338.

Hackman, J. R. (1998). Why teams don't work. In R. S. Tindale, L. Heath, J. Edwards, E. J. Posavac, F. B. Bryant, Y. Suarez-Balcazar, & J. Myers (Eds.), *Theory and research on small groups* (pp. 245–267). New York: Plenum Press.

Hackman, J. R., & Wageman, R. (2005). A theory of team coaching. *The Academy of Management Review, 30*(2), 269–287.

Hennessey, B. A., & Amabile, T. M. (2010). Creativity. *Annual Review of Psychology, 61*(1), 569–598.

Katzenbach, J. R., & Smith, D. K. (1993). The discipline of teams. *Harvard Business Review, 71* (2), 111–120.

Keith, M., Anderson, G., Dean, D. L., & Gaskin, J. (2014). The effects of team flow on performance: A video game experiment. In *Proceedings of SIGHCI 2014*. Paper 13. Retrieved from http://aisel.aisnet.org/sighci2014/13.

Kozlowski, S. W. J., & Klein, K. J. (2000). A multilevel approach to theory and research in organizations: Contextual, temporal, and emergent processes. In K. J. Klein & S. W. J. Kozlowski (Eds.), *Multilevel theory, research, and methods in organizations: Foundations, extensions, and new directions* (pp. 3–90). San Francisco, CA: Jossey-Bass.

Landhäußer, A., & Keller, J. (2012). Flow and its affective, cognitive, and performance-related consequences. In S. Engeser (Ed.), *Advances in flow research* (pp. 65–85). New York: Springer.

Larson, J. R. (2010). *In search of synergy in small group performance*. New York, NY: Psychology Press.

Lencioni, P. M. (2002). *The five dysfunctions of a team*. San Fransisco: Jossey-Bass.

Lyubomirsky, S., King, L., & Diener, E. (2005). The benefits of frequent positive affect: Does happiness lead to success? *Psychological Bulletin, 131*(6), 803–855.

Magyaródi, T., & Oláh, A. (2015). Flow Szinkronizáció Kérdőív: az optimális élmény mechanizmusának mérése társas interakciós helyzetekben. *Mentálhigiéné és Pszichoszomatika, 16*(3), 271–296.

Mantere, S. (2008). Role expectations and middle manager strategic agency. *Journal of Management Studies, 45*(2), 294–316.

Marotto, M., Roos, J., & Victor, B. (2007). Collective virtuosity in organizations: A study of peak performance in an orchestra. *Journal of Management Studies, 44*(3), 388–413.

Nakamura, J., & Csíkszentmihályi, M. (2009). Flow theory and research. In C. R. Snyder & S. J. Lopez (Eds.), *The Oxford handbook of positive psychology* (2nd ed., pp. 195–206). Oxford: Oxford University Press.

Richter, A. W., Dawson, J. F., & West, M. A. (2011). The effectiveness of teams in organizations: a meta-analysis. *The International Journal of Human Resource Management, 22*(13), 2749–2769.

Rousseau, D. M. (1997). Organizational behavior in the new organizational era. *Annual Review of Psychology, 48*(1), 515–546.

Salanova, M., Rodríguez-Sánchez, A. M., Schaufeli, W. B., & Cifre, E. (2014). Flowing together: A longitudinal study of collective efficacy and collective flow among workgroups. *The Journal of Psychology, 148*(4), 435–455.

Salas, E., & Cannon-Bowers, J. A. (2001). The science of training: a decade of progress. *Annual Review of Psychology, 52*(1), 471–499.

Sawyer, R. K. (2003). *Group creativity: Music, theater, collaboration*. Mahwah, NJ: Lawrence Erlbaum Associates.

Sawyer, R. K. (2006). Group creativity: Musical performance and collaboration. *Psychology of Music, 34*(2), 148–165.

Sawyer, R. K. (2007). *Group genius: The creative power of collaboration*. New York: Basic Books.

Snow, K. Y. (2010). *Work relationships that flow: Examining the interpersonal flow experience, knowledge sharing, and organizational commitment*. Doctoral Dissertation. Claremont Graduate University. Retrieved from http://gradworks.umi.com/34/36/3436590.html.

Steiner, I. D. (1972). *Group processes and productivity*. New York: Academic Press.

Van den Hout, J. J. J. (2016). *Team flow: From concept to application*. Dissertation. Eindhoven: Eindhoven University of Technology.

van den Hout, J. J., Davis, O. C., & Weggeman, M. C. (2018). The conceptualization of team flow. *The Journal of Psychology, 152*(6), 388–423.

Van den Hout, J. J. J., Gevers, J. M. P., Davis, O. C., & Weggeman, M. C. D. P. (2017). Overcoming impediments to team flow. *Challenging Organisations and Society, 6*(2), 1165–1181.

Van den Hout, J. J. J., Gevers, J. M. P., Davis, O. C., & Weggeman, M. C. D. P. (2019). Developing and Testing the Team Flow Monitor (TFM). Cogent Psychology, Accepted manuscript, 1643962. https://doi.org/10.1080/23311908.2019.1643962

Verhoeven, B. (2018). *Let's flow! Transformational leadership and team effectiveness: The mediating role of team flow in organizations*. Master Thesis. Eindhoven: Eindhoven University of Technology.

Walker, C. J. (2010). Experiencing flow: Is doing it together better than doing it alone? *The Journal of Positive Psychology, 5*(1), 3–11.

Weggeman, M. C. D. P., Lammers, I., & Akkermans, H. (2007). Aesthetics from a design perspective. *Journal of Organizational Change Management, 20*(3), 346–358.

Wooldridge, B., Schmid, T., & Floyd, S. W. (2008). The middle management perspective on strategy process: Contributions, synthesis, and future research. *Journal of Management, 34*(6), 1190–1221.

Wright, T. A., & Cropanzano, R. (2004). The role of psychological well-being in job performance: A fresh look at an age-old quest. *Organizational Dynamics, 33*(4), 338–351.

Zumeta, L., Basabe, N., Wlodarzyk, A., Bobowik, M., & Paez, D. (2016). Shared flow and positive collective gatherings. *Anales de Psicologia, 32*(3), 717–727. https://doi.org/10.6018/analesps.32.3.261651.

Chapter 4
Exemplifying Team Flow Experiences

4.1 Introduction

After the exhaustive descriptions of flow and team flow of the previous chapters, this chapter will describe some real-world examples. We will show how individual flow experiences can merge during interactions with other people. According to our team flow theory, the experience of team flow is always a result of individual flow experiences that entangle to become something greater. In his book about flow, Csíkszentmihályi gives several examples of flow experiences in teams, such as surgeons, basketball players, and mountaineers.

4.2 Interactions that Perpetuate Flow

While visiting the first World Congress on Positive Psychology in Philadelphia in 2009 (where the authors met), Jef told a cab driver that he was studying flow. This prompted the driver to share his own experience on a merchant ship that reminded him of what Jef was trying to explain. "Whenever I'd been out to sea for a while and I saw a lighthouse, I would feel myself become one with the turning light, especially when it would slowly draw closer, making me feel like part of an enormous, harmonious system." This is a typical example of an individual flow experience containing interactions with larger systems: the rhythmic flashing of the light house, in this case. The difference with teams is that people play off each other, making for much more dynamic interactions.

Any collaboration can be viewed as a set of interactions between two or more people. In an interview, Joseph Oubelkas clearly described what interactions can accomplish. An *interaction* with someone else can keep you focused on what's good. Take Joseph Oubelkas: his interactions with his mother during his 5-year false imprisonment in a Moroccan jail were essential to his survival. Joseph's

Jef J. J. van den Hout and O. C. Davis, *Team Flow*, SpringerBriefs in Well-Being and Quality of Life Research, https://doi.org/10.1007/978-3-030-27871-7_4

mother told us: "Joseph's friends and I would go to help him. We wanted to get him out of prison in the best physical and emotional health possible. The interaction came from those letters. He couldn't let himself become lost in that dark place when he had done nothing wrong." Joseph's reaction to this was:

> "This support, this positive attitude and amazing care is what sustained me as I rebuilt a life behind bars. I had nothing there. Just me. But as long as you control your own body, you have power. So I took good care of myself. Started teaching language classes, built a garden and coached sports. It was tough, but it stopped my life from becoming meaningless" (Oubelkas, 2018).

Joseph made sure he did what was right so that his life could retain meaning and he could still experience moments of flow. Obviously, we can't describe the interactions with his mother in terms of team flow or dyadic flow, but this story is a powerful example of how positive interactions are.

Interactions between master and apprentice can also promote flow. Famous harmonica player Toots Tielemans once taught a single lesson to Tim Welvaars. He taught Welvaars things the latter had never heard in all his years at the academy. "He told me to learn to feel a tone by playing it for 10 min straight. 'You'll *become* the tone,' he said. 'Your body will vibrate along with the tone and once you have a feeling for that vibration, whatever you play will sound great.'" Welvaars believes that was the secret to Toots' success. "He was a very sensitive man. He could feel the tones. That's why he could find the beautiful melodies he did." Toots also taught him many combinations of note progressions. "He taught me combinations that make improvisations interesting. I had never learned to do that on harmonica." (NOS, 2016) Welvaars' experiences illustrate the contagious nature of flow, as well as providing more evidence (if more were needed) that our thoughts, desires and emotions all become one during a flow experience.

4.3 Examples from the World of Business

4.3.1 Philips' Invention of the CD as an Emerging Collective Ambition

The Netherlands has a proud tradition of innovation: the Delta Works, the compact disc, speed cameras. Inventions like these are vitally important and reveal a collective ambition. These kinds of innovations solve problems, make life easier, and bolster the economy. Documentary filmmaker Floris Alberse also saw the importance of innovation, but no one was talking about how to make innovation happen. He went looking for answers from the now-elderly inventors of the CD. These pensioners formed a team back in the day. To explain how their team was so very successful, they pointed to the fact that the team was formed around an idea that was keeping everyone up at night. From this idea, a clear goal had to be formulated. Additionally, leadership had to take a personal interest in the project. What the team needed next was to be left alone by upper management, to buckle down and focus. During the project, the team patiently worked towards the goal, keeping a broad view and an open mind the whole time, always prepared for the unexpected. They questioned their deeply rooted assumptions and suspended their judgement.

This neatly reflects the characteristics of team flow. The team sets a shared goal and starts innovating. The work requires both concentration and collaboration, increasing the odds and incidence of team flow. Comparing this to the team flow theory described in Chap. 3, we can see clear parallels that strongly imply that team flow experiences abounded during the invention of the compact disc.

*4.3.2 Collaborating on MINDF*CK*

Another example of innovation is the work of Victor Mids, real name Victor Middelkoop, a Dutch illusionist, tv producer, and medical doctor. Victor Mids is not a practicing physician, but claims to use his understanding of the brain and senses to fuel his illusions. Before each new season of his show MINDF*CK, Victor Mids and his team face the challenge of coming up with original ideas with which to amaze and confuse their audience. They told us the following about their approach:

> We're very professional about our processes at MINDF*CK. When we're creating a new season, we rent out a villa for a week. We take a team of five to brainstorm around the pool. Everyone can suggest any illusion that seems interesting to them. 'Let's change water into wine!' someone will say. 'Or make the moon disappear!' We come up with tons of ideas this way. Next, we'll come up with a way to do it. Should we use a helicopter and a black screen? Build a replica of the whole thing? Do we hypnotize someone? From there, we'll decide on the best possible solution and how to make it look great. So it all starts from a core concept. Something you can explain in a single sentence. If it takes more than that, the idea's just not good enough.

For things to unfold "in flow" during the performance of the illusion, it is essential for everyone to know exactly where everyone else is, even without looking. The team's cordial working relationship becomes clear from the following interview quote:

> They're my best friends. Have been since childhood. My director, Oscar Verpoort, is my best friend from high school. He and I came up with MINDF*CK together. I can have conversations with Oscar without saying a word. Every illusion has a hidden back end that I'm constantly thinking about. They also have a front, which is what you get to see. The two have to move in parallel. The entire back end happens in flow, allowing the front to look spontaneous. Working with Oscar, I only ever think about the back end. He knows exactly where my head is at and knows instantly when anything goes wrong.

What you can clearly see here is a "merging of action and awareness," a characteristic of individual flow. Spontaneous, controlled action is clearly prevalent here, even at the team level. You might say the team's collective awareness is merging with their joint coordinated actions. This is perhaps the single most typical element of the team flow experience and can be considered a summary or summation of all seven prerequisites and all four characteristics.

4.3.3 Transparency as a Catalyst for Team Flow at Philips

In an interview with Han Schaminée, former business unit director at Philips, we discussed an important flow experience in his career. Han Schaminée was called upon to remediate teams at Philips. In the middle of all this, there was still a new TV-set in need of developing. In spite of his foreboding mission statement, Han still managed to raise the teams he worked with to new heights. He achieved this by communicating transparently and by aligning the employees' personal goals. This alignment he accomplished by announcing to the teams that they would be terminated, but that if they worked hard, they could move to another position at Philips. The use of open communication allowed everyone involved to realize that close cooperation would be in everyone's best interest. The teams rallied around their personal ambition to find work within Philips and excelled. The improvement to team communication soon led to better inter-team communication and optimized workflows. Initial successes started rolling in, reinforcing the sense that they could achieve their shared goal. This was partially due to some excellent feedback from within the organization keeping them informed and on track. This gave the teams a sense of being "state of the art," which helped them feel secure in their ability to achieve their objectives. As people came to trust themselves, so did they come to trust each other, growing to realize that they needed each other to reach the shared goal.

It was a roaring success in the end. A new TV-set was developed and everyone found a new position thanks to their efforts and achievements. In retrospect, their reactions may seem fueled by fear, but closer examination rules that out. It was open communication and a sense of security that allowed the team members to trust each other completely and collaborate effectively (and transcend the fear of failure!). There was a common goal that everyone agreed with and to which everyone had aligned their personal goal of staying employed at Philips. They needed each other to reach that goal, and reach it they did. Look up members of that team today and they will tell you about this experience in some detail. Team spirit on the project was astronomical and everyone involved was immensely proud of what they accomplished together. Their story reflects many elements of team flow (aligned goals, collective goals, security, open communication and mutual trust) and is a fine example of how team flow allows teams to reach new heights of achievement.

4.3.4 *Trust as a Building Block for Team Flow at Buurtzorg (in-Home Care)*

We found another fine example of team flow in our conversations with an employee of Buurtzorg Nederland (a Dutch organization providing in-home care to the elderly and infirm). Buurtzorg Nederland has gathered international acclaim as a high-performing healthcare organization whose employees work in self-managed teams and find their work extremely satisfying. Three members of Buurtzorg Nederland's Zelhem team spoke to us about their team flow experiences.

From our conversations, we gathered that the employees found the innovative organizational structure liberating. Employees are given as much personal responsibility as they can handle, which immediately improves their job satisfaction. For that very reason, Buurtzorg tends to attract workers who are keen to try new things and unafraid to take on new responsibilities. These qualities are required, as they have to run in-home care for the surrounding area by themselves. That also requires a lot of collaboration. These freedoms allow team members to be their authentic selves and perform optimally. Sharing all responsibility has often proven a catalyst for team flow experiences. These highly trained people divide their tasks among themselves in a way that allows each member to do what they're best at and what they most enjoy doing, making the most of the skills and abilities present in the team. The team members share a bond of trust that is especially important when adversity strikes, which in this line of work can be a matter of life and death. This trust means each member has people to turn to, which is essential in any strong team and a requirement for experiencing team flow. Open communication also contributes to the success of Buurtzorg's teams. When something challenging happens, help is promptly requested and immediately offered. The team members can be vulnerable around each other without fear that their trust will be violated. Everyone is considered to hold equal value and authority, which is not a claim many organizations can make. This equality aids open communication, which in turn contributes to team flow. Finally, there are frequent team meetings as well as constant casual consultations, ensuring that everyone knows what everyone else is doing and how to help each other when needed. This allows them not only to provide better care to their clients, but to do more as a team than anyone thought possible.

Clearly, Buurtzorg teams exhibit all of the elements of team flow described in Chap. 2. We talked to many employees from many different Buurtzorg teams. Time and again, we encountered teams bursting with positivity, where employees truly enjoyed and excelled at their work. For that reason, Buurtzorg warrants further discussion, and we'll use it as example in Chap. 6, where we will describe its organizational structure in detail.

4.4 Examples from the Music Industry

The following two examples show team flow in action on stage. They show how band members can complement each other and how the collective result transcends the individual. In his book *Life*, Keith Richards of the Rolling Stones describes, in typical team flow terms, how the team arrives at true beauty together and how that leads to moments of elation:

> You'll be sitting around playing with a couple of guys and think: ooh, yeah! That feeling is more valuable than anything. At some point you'll realize that you have briefly transcended the world, that you can't be touched. You're floating, because you're hanging out with a couple of guys who want to do the same thing you do. And when it works, baby, you grow wings. You'll know you're in a place few people will ever reach; you're somewhere truly special. And you'll want to keep going back up there, knowing you'll be arrested when you land. But you'll always want to go back up there. It's flying without a license.

Richards's example provides a moving description of the feeling of making progress together. In team flow, this is often accompanied by a sense of rising, of being lifted up, as well as feelings of transcendence (cf. Eisenberg, 1990). These feelings come from being part of something larger than oneself (the band, in Richards's case), which is already included in the team flow model under the header of *a sense of unity*. Also reported are feelings of elevation (Haidt, 2000), the sensation of floating experienced in a group setting because the group is doing something worthwhile together. You're building on each other's abilities, which creates a sense of joint progress. People often report a feeling of enormous gratitude for being able to rely on the skills and support provided by their teammates. We don't consider this sense of gratitude a required element of team flow, more of a bonus that shows up when activities include an element of beauty (like making music) or during moments of reflection on team activities. The same feeling shows up in professional environments, where it is usually labeled synergy (cf. Kurtzberg & Amabile, 2001). The sense of making progress together also indicates that the optimal balance has been struck between autonomy (each team member is counted) and alignment (everyone contributes). What's important in both cases is the sense of making progress on an activity together. That feeling is essential to the experience of team flow and is often accompanied by other positive feelings, like fulfilment. The absence of progress can be enormously frustrating and that frustration often comes with additional bad feelings.

How teams align their efforts to achieve synergy was explained beautifully by Steve Jobs in an interview with 60 min.

> The Beatles are my business model: four talented individuals compensating for each other's weaknesses and creating balance and harmony together. The whole was greater than the sum of its parts. Their synergy was the magic. As a team, the Beatles performed incredibly innovating experiments. After the break-up, they still made good stuff, but they never reached that level again."

4.5 Examples Based on Sports

There's nothing wrong with a little ego in the group, but it's important to position those egos where they can be functional. Of course, it would be ideal if the team's star player were humble. Here's what Gareth Bale had to say in a press conference after Wales beat Belgium in the 2016 European Championship:

> The team is the star first. There is no stars in our team, we are all together. We all work as one, we all run for each other, we all attack for each other, we fight for each other, we are just a very close team, we all get along like brothers, we all joke and laugh and mess around, as you sure have seen on social media and everything. We are here having fun, we are here enjoying the occasion.

You could tell that this team was in flow together. Their interactions were all very positive and they were clearly having fun, as indeed were their Welsh supporters. Bale's quote also reflects his belief in putting the team first. He has no interest in putting himself forward, because that could harm the team's unity.

4.5.1 Cycling

The fact that team flow is a more intense experience than individual flow was affirmed in a television interview with a Dutch cyclist. This cyclist made the following spot-on comment after his team won the time trials: "When you have your own plan and it works out, that's great. But if you have a plan with a team and it works out, that's obviously phenomenal!" This implies that experiencing flow in a team is even more intense than experiencing it on your own. People enjoy reaching a shared goal more than they enjoy achieving a personal one. The likely reason for this is the fact that the team sacrificed and labored for each other, helped each other along and now shares both the victory and its (emotional) rewards, inducing both gratitude and elation.

4.5.2 Soccer

In a biographical issue on former international soccer player Wim Kieft, author Michel van Egmond brings up the season of play during which Kieft regularly entered flow thanks to his highly experienced teammates and the general atmosphere in the team. Here's what the man himself had to say:

> What could be better for a player than to be the best, to make the calls, to be fit and ready to shine? Isn't it fantastic to do something you're good at, to be able to rely completely on your skills and talent? Those are cherished memory for me: the matches that went smoothly, where I didn't have to think, where everything seemed to be happening by itself. I had a few runs like that, where every header would connect and I was never in the wrong

> position. Those were magical times, I think. You could feel perfectly free in matches like that. I had that sense very strongly in my first season at PSV, after my return from France. I was returning to Eindhoven in great shape to a strong, well-practiced team and felt perfectly at ease. I never felt too pressured, my teammates were willing to put their faith in me, and I had a really easy time scoring goals. That was a joyful, carefree season. It's one of a very few seasons where I really dared to be myself on the pitch. (Van Egmond, 2014)

The sense of freedom he talks about shows that his team found the optimal balance between interdependence and autonomy, as discussed earlier in the Rolling Stones example and in Chap. 3. The freedom to do what you know you can do well in a team is extremely conducive to team flow. The quote also mentions how being trusted by your coach and teammates and being surrounded by competent teammates whom you trust can really help put your mind at ease, giving you more space to experience individual flow during matches. And for an entire season, no less.

4.5.3 Volleyball

One final moment of team flow we want to share comes from Wim Koch, former team coach and, at the time of our interview, director of the sports center at the Eindhoven University of Technology. He describes a match between Hajraa and Peelpush, teams in the Netherlands's 2nd division C. The specific moment we want to discuss happened in the final and deciding match of the championship in May of 2000. What we will describe below shows how important open, positive, direct, and constructive communication is. It also shows the benefits of a coach who actively involves the team in its own training program and match preparations and then deliberately takes a step back during matches. Here is what Wim Koch told us in his interview:

> It was the final match in the competition and there was only a single point in it between us and our opponents. Whoever won this match would be promoted into the 1st division, just below the premier league. Throughout the year, we had been working to analyze plays on paper and on video. The players could see at a glance what they needed to work on and they knew how to improve. They were highly skilled at reviewing analyses and getting the most out of them. That's vital in a match where the standards are this high.
>
> As soon as the match began, one player immediately blocked the ball straight down, scoring with a beautiful one-man block. Our opponents took an ego hit right out of the gate. Our player flashed me a thumbs-up and I relaxed, confident we would do well. I sat back to enjoy the match. The boys were in flow. I was in flow. From that moment on, everyone knew that they had prepared right and everyone knew what they needed to do strategically. In a technical sense, too, they were at the top of their game after years of training to perform certain actions flawlessly. But it was mostly the strategic preparations that ensured the team knew exactly what needed to happen and was able to adapt quickly to changing circumstances. This gave them tons of confidence and motivation, a real killer mentality.
>
> We stayed in flow for the entire match and because we could just be who we were as a team, we kept scoring. There's no arguing with the results. We beat them a solid three-nil in sets, with scores of 15-3, 15-7 and 15-2.

> There were a few reasons we entered flow in this match. First, the team members were technically and tactically prepared to carry out the game plan. This wouldn't have been possible were it not for the analyses we conducted, in which we reviewed video with each team member and used that to provide feedback and plan training exercises. The analysis was done and discussed with individuals, but each individual's improved skills had an immediate effect on the team. The team members also had to learn to work with these analyses so that they would understand the information and know how to apply it on the court. This gave the team members the sense that they were capable of winning. That's the feeling a coach is supposed to instill in his team. We constantly told each player what they were good at; their best qualities and skills. The team members also need to believe in the match strategy, that it will help them win and that they can carry it to fruition. This sense needs to start well ahead of the match, in preparation and in training. That takes a lot of time. Repetition is key, and the visual aspect is vitally important.
>
> Finally, it's crucial for the team to experience in real life that they can succeed and that the strategy can work. When it comes time to execute and what you've been preparing works, and is recognized to work, then the whole team finds confidence that the whole plan will work. The members of my team saw on that court that every technical and tactical element of the game plan they had prepared worked. That basically made them unbeatable.
>
> The team will take that and run with it. Nothing more for a coach to do.
>
> The contribution of the players themselves to a flow experience is enormous. As their coach, you provide advice, point things out to them, but in the end the players need to manage each other. The game shifts so quickly that there's no way for a coach to follow along and shout instructions. The players need to pick up on the play and adapt on the fly. Communication, clear instructions and calling each other out on mistakes is what keeps the whole team sharp. When you call someone out though, it's important to tell them how they can do better. There's no point telling people they're doing it wrong and leaving it at that. Interaction between the players and myself is also important, and you have to make yourself available for that. Players can have great ideas and sometimes come up with surprising solutions. As a coach, your job is to vet and mold their ideas so they mesh with your overall tactical concept for the team. Incorporating these ideas gives players the sense that they contributed meaningfully to the team's style of play.
>
> Assigning responsibility to the players is a way of making them manage themselves and their teammates. Honestly, that is a professional athlete's strength, really. You can't always tie them to exact responses to specific situations. You need to give pros the opportunity to create their own solutions, which means keeping a light touch on the tiller.

The preceding paragraphs cover every single prerequisite of team flow. We can see that thorough preparation in which all of the team's strengths are discussed is important in order to bring all the available talent together on the court. It's essential to involve the players themselves in the analysis and to let them arrive at new understanding on their own. These pre-match analyses build mutual trust and a belief that this team and these people can prevail. During the match, this dynamic creates the sense of making progress together as the team's preparation starts paying off. You can also see that there is attention for the individual, that each member is assigned a clear task, allowing for the experience of individual flow, which contributes to the team's experience. This is further confirmation that team flow arises from individual contributions that can themselves ignite individual flow experiences. We can also see that both the team and its members bear responsibility for the outcome and are given as much space as possible to come up with their own solutions. Wim Koch believes this to be essential. Professional athletes share responsibility for the team's success as well as their own, and each team member can be held personally accountable by any other. Only when the team feels this autonomy and agrees completely on the chosen tactics can the team experience flow together. In the team flow model, this tactical agreement is represented by the seven prerequisites of team flow.

References

Eisenberg, E. M. (1990). Jamming transcendence through organizing. *Communication Research, 17*(2), 139–164.

Haidt, J. (2000). The positive emotion of elevation. *Prevention and Treatment, 3*(3), 1–5. http://faculty.virginia.edu/haidtlab/articles/haidt.2000.the-positive-emotion-of-elevation.pub020.pdf.

Kurtzberg, T. R., & Amabile, T. M. (2001). From Guilford to creative synergy: Opening the black box of team-level creativity. *Creativity Research Journal, 13*(3–4), 285–294.

NOS. (2016). https://nos.nl/artikel/2127649-toots-vroeg-me-wat-wil-je-weten-ik-zei-alles.html. Retrieved on August 22, 2016.

Van Egmond, M. (2014). *Kieft*. Amsterdam: A.W. Bruna Uitgevers.

Chapter 5
Impediments to Team Flow Experiences

The construct of team flow can be more easily described than created for many work teams, both because many of the antecedents are hard to generate and because there are a host of roadblocks that can stand between a team and its flow. In this chapter, we will review both the barriers teams face as they pursue flow experiences, and the pitfalls that lurk along the way.

5.1 How to Build a Bad Team

One of the biggest problems that ruins a team is ad hoc composition. Instead of building a team from people who buy into its purpose, or who possess relevant skills and interests, or who work well with each other, or who actually want to be on this project, teams are put together because people happen to be available at the right time, or because a team "needs" a person from a given division. Whenever a team is put together without careful consideration and deliberate selection of its members, it is starting at a disadvantage. It also helps to make sure that it is very clear who is actually on the team, as research by Wageman, Hackman, and Lehman (2005) found that teams can set what they consider to be clear membership boundaries and still have disagreement among individual members about who is actually on which team!

The question of who will "work well" together, though, is often more of a puzzler than one might expect. When everyone in the group is highly agreeable, it can be easy to reach consensus, but it is just as easy to devolve into groupthink. Similarly, putting friendly coworkers together on a team because of their friendliness can instantiate some happiness, but it can also lead to their pairing off, excluding people, and/or arguing as a bloc. Granted, no one wants problematic people on the team, but it can be worthwhile to have opinionated and perhaps even disagreeable people on the team (NB: disagreeable is not the same as being uncivil). The question is not one of team happiness or team affability. It is one of cohesion, which (as mentioned) is about the psychological safety to voice one's ideas and

Jef J. J. van den Hout and O. C. Davis, *Team Flow*, SpringerBriefs in Well-Being and Quality of Life Research, https://doi.org/10.1007/978-3-030-27871-7_5

trusting that all team members are aligned with the goal and will work to their highest abilities.

The dangerous other side of the "work well together" question is too much focus on the individual. A lot of the training and development initiatives that human resource departments create focus on the skills of individuals, and even team building workshops are directed at general team participation skills rather than focusing on how a particular team gets on. Similarly, coaching too often focuses exclusively upon the individual without regard for the dynamics that exist between the individual and the other team members. And then there are the accursed personality tests, which often serve teams about as well as their horoscopes. Whatever a person may or may not be like in general does not fully (or even reasonably) predict how they will act in a particular context—for instance, introverts can be very talkative with the right group even if they're quiet in most. Skillsets and working styles, too, are often selected at the individual level without consideration for how they will apply at the group level, in particular how they will mesh with the skills and methods of others.

Of course, there is some merit to team training, especially when you are working on training a specific set of people to work together. But that in no way suggests that you need to be doing trust falls and rope courses to teach people how to be interdependent. Cheesy ice breakers run the risk of hardening the frost by inhibiting participation, and silly games might get people laughing together, but they do not necessarily get them *working* together. The best introductions revolve around building consensus around the team's goals and purpose, assessing whether everyone can contribute to that purpose both together and separately, and identifying whether anyone has particular needs that must be met in order for them to participate fully (and whether the team can meet them).

Similarly, the purpose underlying the team's existence must be selected with intention, not just in light of the company's goals, but in light of who may be available to fulfill the aims of the intended project. One should consider whether fulfilling the purpose actually requires a team, or whether it can be accomplished by people working in parallel, individuals or dyads handing off pieces of the project to others, or completed *in toto* by just one or two people. In order to coalesce a team around a project, the goals must be clear enough to select people carefully and have those people buy in, which stands in contrast to how teams often face a vague mission like "design a new product" or "fix the bugs in the system" (is it a bug or is it a feature?). Sometimes, the team is convened to achieve a vague goal (e.g., "make the machine work like this") with a view to their clarifying what the actual problem is (and thus what the goal should be), only to find that increasing clarity on the problem also highlights the fact that the wrong people were invited to the meeting. The result is frustration, distrust of the managers that called in the team, and greater difficulty keeping people engaged.

Picking the wrong leader for the team is just as bad. You can get the right talent in the room, give them a clear, meaningful goal, and then stick a dinosaur brain at the head of the table. You know the type: it roars loudly, ignores what people say, does what it wants, stomps around looking to see what it can snag, and generally makes a nuisance of itself. Sometimes it is just about ego, or worse, a rock star with an ego, or someone whose professional goals do not align with the team's, or who has a leadership style that does not mesh well with the team's dynamic. The leader could be from a place in the company that offers the leader less familiarity with the constraints of the project/team, or whose department is at cross purposes the department creating the team. Whatever the case: bad leader, bad team.

Cross purposes are a subset of the team-busting horror called *politics*, and it is a bugbear to any team. Ideally, the team should have no politics within it, no politics brought to bear upon any member of the team, and no politics bearing down upon the team from the outside. Besides putting people at cross purposes, there are several key ways in which politics destroy a team. One is limiting the team's resources, because the various teams and departments in the company are all trying to get their hands on a limited budget. A second is putting people on a team because of their title, position, or for fear of excluding them, rather than including them because they can contribute uniquely and effectively to the team. Another, which is more of a silent killer, is the pressure that inhibits risk-taking. If any stakeholders connected to the team are loath to stick their necks out and take what they consider to be a smart risk, then progress can be stalled either for a time or for good (perhaps we should say: for worse). Ideally, it is the job of the team's creator to shield the team from any adverse effects that come from politics. The more day-to-day reality deviates from that ideal, the greater the risk of doom for the team's objectives.

As noted above, buy-in and clarity are critical parts of forming a team. The entity forming the team can have a clear idea about the goal, carefully select the right people, block out the politics, choose the right leader, get everyone in the room, and then watch all hell break loose because the goal was not transmitted clearly and/or was not accepted by the members of the team. Just because one person convened a team for what they thought was a clear purpose, doesn't mean the whole team will be on the same page, or that they will consider the goal to be meaningful, achievable, and worthwhile. Once the team is called together, it is important for the goal not to be dictated to them so much as offered to them as a starting point for discussion. In that way, the team can weigh in about the goals, opt in or out (which has to be allowed), and even bring in additional people for consultation. The reality, however, is that teams are often brought together in a rush, given little time to discuss their goals, and confined to the team regardless of their opinion about whether they should be present and/or whether others should be along for the ride. There's nothing like starting off a project believing it makes no sense, has nothing to do with you, lacks the people and resources it needs, or shouldn't even be happening!

The last major error that can torpedo a team before it leaves the harbor is presuming that a virtual team works as well as an in-person team. Plainly: it doesn't. To paraphrase Aragorn (in Peter Jackson's *The Lord of the Rings: Return of the King*): there may come a day when technology lets us see people in as much detail and context as we would get in a meeting room, but it is not this day. And there may come a day when collaboration tools are seamless, and we can both work on the same documents in real time while being wholly visible to one another as if we were side by side, but it is not this day. This day we are isolated! And when we treat virtual teams like live ones, we knowingly remove context and detail from the trust-building moments of introductions, and so compromise them along with the potential for psychological safety. Teams can work virtually once they have met, but they still must meet in person at least once, and should continue to have opportunities to meet in person throughout the project.

5.2 How to Mess up a Great Team

Let us suppose that you convened a team around a purpose, chose members carefully to each make a unique and meaningful contribution, let them confer, review, polish, and buy into the team's goals, gave them the opportunity to review team membership and alter things as they collectively see fit, shielded them from political fallout, and gave them *carte blanche* to acquire the resources they need. You have now successfully gotten to the first minute of real teamwork; you're off to the races! It is astounding how quickly things can go wrong, however.

There's any number of places where the rot can set in, but a notable one is the follow-through. It is one thing to commit to doing tasks and quite another to deliver on that commitment. As people start the task, make progress, and start encountering the unforeseen, things can start to go wrong: time conflicts, incorrect estimates about needed resources (including time/energy), specifications that don't quite fit what is actually needed or wanted, people who discover a need to change directions, changing priorities, new tasks, breakdowns, *et cetera*. Suddenly, plans go out the window and deliverables go undelivered, often for good reasons and despite the best intentions. These dropped balls become tests of whether there is tolerance for failure, suitable procedures for accountability, and trust. No matter how much preparation has been made in those areas, they can be badly strained, and the team will need to band together to handle problems in real time and put out fires as they occur. This will involve switching tasks, helping others at the expense of one's own work, spending time waiting (or tolerating the added strain of task switching so as not to waste time), etc. Team members need to actually be as supportive of one another as they planned to be while still holding each other to the agreed-upon plans and standards.

As surely as there will be mistakes and accidents, there will be miscommunications. A said one thing, B heard another, and both thought that the message was sent and received correctly. As soon as that happens, all hell can break loose. It can happen when C jumps in and takes a side and then A/B feel like it's suddenly two against one. Another source of communication problems is the blame game (see Dattner and Dahl, 2012, on how to avoid this), at which point a lot of time and energy is wasted on figuring out who is responsible for the misunderstanding rather than accepting that it can happen between two honest, earnest, well-meaning people and that the focus needs to be upon working out the current situation. Here, again, fault tolerance is needed. The challenge is that fault tolerance, and the prerequisite trust, are built slowly, and are built most strongly when the team survives something going disastrously wrong.

A similar problem shows up when people start to question whether the realities of the team's tasks and interactions are what they signed up for. And sometimes they're not. This is a case where the team needs to band together so that they can smooth the rough edges and make sure that everyone is getting what they need. Too often, the response to these concerns is to 'just suck it up.' This is an unhelpful attempt to avoid putting in the time and energy to validate people's concerns, find out which of their needs are not being met, which of their expectations have been violated, and to create a bespoke solution. This is penny wise, pound foolish. By "saving" this time and expense, you create antagonism and potentially prompt sabotage through inaction or (if the person is mad, disillusioned, or disenfranchised enough) even overt action, which will waste far more time and resources. This sort of short-sighted thinking is common, and fails to recognize that every team member occasionally needs a pep talk, a reframing of commitment and tasks, and/or a review of what needs to be done. Maintaining commitment is paramount, but that takes time, effort, energy, and sometimes money that people think a team should not have to spend. Some people think that they can incite, or even force, someone to "take one for the team." Taking one for the team is a charitable act of personal sacrifice. When it's forced, it's called scapegoating and comes at a high price.

Unfortunately, new problems can sometimes mean that people might "need" to switch in and out of the team. This should be avoided at almost any cost once the team has developed a dynamic that works, and many teams and managers are too quick to make substitutions rather than help the team stay together and keep its groove. That is not to say that switches should never happen, but they should occur only because of a major event (e.g., someone left the company). When people sit in fear that they could be kicked off the team for any infraction, they lose trust and become risk-averse, which means that they will try to conform to the team's opinion, not speak up, and do only what they need to in attempt not to stand out and run the risk of ridicule and ejection. Needless to say, culture plays a major role in this, and needs to be carefully considered when dealing with diverse and international teams.

Just as infractions are not necessarily fatal to a team or its members, so too is conflict not necessarily a problem. In fact, it is frequently a good thing! It's the fear of disagreement, discomfort with conflict, and the pressure to maintain group unity that can incite people to think of conflict as a problem. In turn, this can lead to one or more people avoiding conflict, or leaders trying to suppress conflict, which can lead to groupthink and artificial consensus. In both cases, this can build private resentment and erode trust from the inside out. Instead, the group needs to make sure it builds and maintains tolerance for conflict, and to handle it by recognizing the need for freewheeling discussion, dissension, and *eventual* consensus. This necessitates productive conflict that is resolved without anyone taking matters personally. Conflict needs to be about finding the best way forward (i.e., a win-win) rather than being a win-lose situation, and those whose ideas are not used or are not fully accepted by the team need to walk away feeling that the team values what they put forward regardless of whether it is used. Anything short of this is a storm that will inevitably rain torrents on the team at an inconvenient time.

One of the main sources of destructive conflict on a team is negativity. First, it is important to realize that negativity is *not* conflict or disagreement per se, but rather offering pessimistic views or critical comments about a person, task, or product/outcome that are not supported by pertinent facts or relevant experience. Examples of negativity include doomsaying, nagging, and complaining, all of which occur without assuming the responsibility of offering solutions. In this, we are indeed pointing out that being unnecessarily negative in the presence of the group is actually *irresponsible*. It wastes time, and it shirks the responsibility to contribute productively to the team. If someone has a well-reasoned critique, then it needs to be welcome, provided it is delivered appropriately and in a timely fashion. But, comments like "That's lousy work," or "What in the @#$% are you doing?" serve only to create animosity, and comments like "I hate doing this part!" bespeak a lack of commitment to the team and its goals. (That said, the scutwork should be parceled out carefully and, when possible, evenly.)

With so many moving parts on a team, it is not so much a matter of *if*, but a matter of *when* a teammate does/says something counterproductive. This is more than making a mistake; it is snapping at a coworker after a 16-h sprint, or being the cause of a tangible setback for the team, doing shoddy work (no matter how good the reason), or accidentally ruining someone else's work in a potentially-preventable way. One might think that the best thing to do is let it go for the sake of team unity, but that lack of accountability is a time bomb that will blow up in the team's face.

One of the foundations of a team's trust is accountability, and that means holding people to their mistakes and requiring that amends be made. If someone is genuinely committed to the team, they will value the opportunity to restore or rebuild their integrity and fix their mistakes. When they do so, it further cements everyone's trust the team member's commitment to fulfilling their duties and the goals of the team. As noted above, however, holding people accountable is going to mean conflict, and it must be done without unproductive blame, and with a presumption of good intentions.

Over the course of the team's mission, there need to be regular check-ins to ensure that each individual's personal goals are also being met. Sure, team members are subordinating their goals to the higher purpose of the team, but that does not mean that they are *forgetting* those goals. A team is give *and take*, and people often forget the second part. People want to derive benefits from participating in a team, and the notion of putting the team first can make people forget that teams are made up of individuals with wants, needs, and hopes. The team needs to be making sure that everyone is "paid" in whatever currency they signed up for, be it recognition, a challenge, or fulfilling an agenda. It is imperative that the team know how each member expects to be paid (beyond remuneration), and to respect that there may need to be regular payouts in the agreed-upon currency. Reneging on this in the name of team unity, as happens frequently, is a recipe for disaster.

5.3 Flow Inhibitors

In addition to the factors that can knock out your team, there are many ways to inhibit participants' individual or joint flow experiences. The focus of this section will be the most important factors likely to disrupt the nine characteristics of individual flow.

One of the primary factors of whether someone experiences flow is clear goals. The team's purpose and objectives may be crystal clear, but if the division of labor leads to murkier goals at the individual level, people will start to disengage. Individuals need a clear goal throughout, as well as some indication that they remain effective (i.e., feedback). Thus, in addition to having accountability in place, it is important for the individual to know the precise metrics by which accountability will occur, and likewise what needs to be done and how that item fits in with what others are doing. One of the most common ways to mess that up is when two people are told to complete a task, and they just look at each other in utter confusion. Worse, people in that position are likely to dive right in and do whatever seems right to them without finding out what everyone else is doing. Avoiding this pitfall requires a clear division of labor that records what each individual and group of individuals in the team is doing, and how their efforts will come together to further the team's agenda.

Another challenge to the experience of flow is *challenge*. Sure, there is scutwork to be done on any project, but it is important to maintain a high challenge level for each member of the team. What tends to happen instead is too much focus on the results instead of the process, and creating something that is "good enough" without regard for who can do more or do better. While the adage "the perfect is the enemy of the good" still applies, the dull is also the enemy of the good. When people do not feel challenged, they get listless, sloppy, and stop acting with diligence. Apathy can set in, causing team members to stop communicating, and stop challenging potential problems. When that happens, you lose a high performer and get a drone instead.

Keeping the work challenging goes hand in hand with taking smart risks, if only because those are fresh, interesting, and different enough to create a challenge. That means psychological safety is also a crucial part of maintaining the challenge level, because people will only stick their necks out if they feel safe. As mentioned above, it is incumbent upon every member of the team to ensure that each of the others is enjoying a challenge, even if that means adding some spice to the scutwork.

Working with a team necessarily involves working under constraints, and this is perfectly fine, as constraints can promote creativity (see Amabile, Conti, Coon, Lazenby, & Herron, 1996, for a discussion). But, constraints can also become overly restrictive, to the point where someone can feel like the team or its members are dictating what they should be doing how and when. When it comes to distributing tasks, there is a fine line between coordination and feeling coerced. Teamwork can quickly devolve into cattiness when people say things like: "You need to do the task this way because that's how I do it." Or even: "The best way to get it done is like this, so why are you doing it that way?" This sort of derision does not promote fellowship feelings, to say the least, but it also leaves people with the sense that they do not have control over their own work. Consistent with the lack of fear of failure in flow experiences, as well as the merging of action and awareness, a person in flow feels a sense of control. It is almost impossible, however, to feel any such sense when facing artificial constraints that have been dictated to you. That goes not just for management, but for coworkers.

People can get trapped in a role as well as in a task. People like to try new things, learn and grow, but being part of a team incurs the risk of being the person who always does a certain task. That does not mean the orchestra's tuba player suddenly wants to play the violin, but it might mean that the tuba player may sometimes want to have a little more of a feature (say, a Shostakovich or Mahler symphony) than it might in some of the major composers' works where it tends to be just a part of orchestra. You might notice that jazz bands, for instance, give each player a cadenza to showcase their skills, usually with some announcement of their name ("Pat Smith on the drums, folks!"), which means that even the drummer, who tends to be viewed as a background player (despite the high difficulty of jazz drumming!), gets the chance to be featured as a lead musician. Every member of the team wants a chance to go beyond their current position in some way, and the team as a whole should create those opportunities and avoid pigeonholing people. The development of individuals has the added benefit of increasing the capacity of the team to tackle ever harder and more interesting challenges.

While it is important to protect the team from political fallout, it is also important to shield them from distractions. Perhaps one of the most stressful markers of adulthood is dealing with a host of competing priorities and being forced to triage. While acknowledging that some trade-offs are necessary, and likewise that factors like work-life balance are crucial to the success of any employee, it is also important to make sure that teamwork is not interrupted by non-team work. When team members are working on team tasks, that needs to be as close to 100% of their focus as possible. Real emergencies happen, but the team needs to protect itself and its members from unnecessary distractions. That can be as simple as allowing team members to mark themselves as out-of-office in the company calendar, or having managers run interference on incoming tasks from other parts of the company, or setting phones on silent in the team room. This notion of being on-call to whoever needs you at whatever time was always a terrible idea (in most jobs), but that goes double (at least) when trying to focus on teamwork. The only way to build synergy and synchrony is to have focus, and to drill down to what contributes to the team. This freedom from distraction is a key component of flow, and must be protected in order for the individuals and the team to perform at their best.

5.4 Impediments to Team Flow

In our own research, we did a study (Van den Hout et al., 2017) across 28 teams to see what was standing between them and team flow. All team members were asked what prevented them from experiencing flow while performing tasks in service of their specific teams. We found that impediments to flow could be organized into four categories.

- **Motivational issues** (co-worker laxity, disengagement)
- **Interpersonal issues** within the process of collaboration (miscommunication, negativity, disagreement, unresolved conflict)
- **Task-related issues** (ambiguity, disorganization, work pressure, lack of challenge)
- **Environmental issues** (distractions)

One of the biggest problems turned out to be accountability. As mentioned above, dropping balls is an individual problem that can affect the team, but at the team-level the problem is more about taking responsibility for dropping the ball. That is, it is incumbent upon the team not to play the blame game, but it is also critical for the person who errs to take responsibility for putting things back together and redoubling their efforts to promote the success of the team.

Where the issue of team and individual accountability can be a real beast is during handoffs. When Alex is assigned a task, he is expected not only to complete it, but to do so in a manner that is consistent with the norms, standards, and related work of the team. A task, however well performed, that cannot be integrated into the rest of the team's work is effectively worthless, and the very act of offering such a product threatens the group's integrity. First, it shows that the person is not thinking about the team's needs and goals (intentionally or not, it's a problem either way); and second, it wastes time and resources. This has the effect of throwing the team off its groove and reminding people of their individuality when they need to be contributing to the group.

An alternate version of the handoff problem is simply giving over a product without consideration for the context in which it is given. Imagine a team juggling balls not only as individuals, but as a group, passing balls around from one member to another while keeping their individual sets in the air. One does not throw a ball to someone else whenever the mood strikes, because that would destroy the entire system. Similarly, one does not just drop a completed task on the table and walk away. It must be presented to those who will use it along with assistance coordinating its use with the stakeholders who will take it as input. That also means the stakeholders need to be able to attend to the coordination, and be ready to use what they receive, and it is the responsibility of the task owner to ensure that all this coordination occurs.

Uncoordinated handoff is one of many examples of the team-level problem of distractions. While it is crucial for the team to be shielded from outside distractions, it is just as important that they work together to ensure that they are not distracting each other. Ironically, these issues fit many of the concerns that relate to an open office plan, such as going over and asking questions without regard for whether someone is busy, watching people unnecessarily, and giving unsolicited comments. It is important to remember that full team flow requires both the team *and the individuals* to be in flow, and that means protecting one another from distractions. This includes being judicious about interruptions and the timing of handoffs, comments, and critiques, because even the most well-done versions of those can be fatal if they cause someone to be distracted.

The discussion of distractions inevitably leads to the biggest time-waster of all: meetings. As Jason Fried pointed out in his TED Talk, Why Work Doesn't Happen at Work:

> Companies often think of a 1-hour meeting as a one-hour meeting, but that's not true, unless there's only one person. If there are 10 people, it's a 10-hour meeting, not a one-hour meeting. It's 10 hours of productivity taken from the rest of the organization to have this one-hour meeting, which probably should have been handled by two or three people talking for a few minutes.

So much team spirit is lost by forcing people to sit through meetings where they do not actually need to know what is going on and they do not feel that they have anything to contribute. To waste people's time like that causes them to feel disrespected and devalued, not to mention distracted, bored, and restless. And who wouldn't question their commitment to a team that requires them to sit through hours of mind-numbing nonsense? Instead, it is important to make sure that everyone who attends a meeting knows why it is happening, has something to hear or say (and agrees that such hearing/saying is necessary), and will actually do measurably better work because of it. And, of course, keep it as short as possible—everyone loves it when meetings end early or on-time! Granted, many teams want to open and close each day with a meeting, and that is fine, but keep them to a maximum of 15 min each—anything longer rarely requires the full team, outside of general brainstorming (which should be done judiciously, carefully, and rarely).

By now, it should go without saying that people really do need to communicate. Unfortunately, there are many times when people shy away from saying what they need to. Fear of asking questions and seeming incompetent, fear of giving feedback and seeming too negative, and fear offering suggestions and provoking "unnecessary" conflict or hurting team cohesion, are all going to be fatal to the team. It is important to remember that both individual and team flow depend upon the individual/team receiving timely and constructive feedback, and that includes criticism and disagreement. Everyone needs to know if and how progress is being achieved at every level (cf. Amabile & Kramer, 2011), and that means knowing both when they are doing well, and when they are going the wrong way. People need to be comfortable speaking to members of the group and/or finding proxies to make sure their voices are heard (like preparing for a team meeting with a colleague who will do the talking for both). This requires both trust and psychological safety. It also means, however, that establishing the team's norms also requires instantiating and reviewing feedback and communication (including listening!) rules/models. It is worthwhile to make sure everyone knows and agrees how and when communication and feedback will take place.

Ultimately, we find that the main inhibitors of the team flow experience were the opposites of the characteristics of team flow. Instead of focus, there are distractions at many levels, both from without and from within. Instead of mutual trust, there is distrust, negativity, lack of personal responsibility, and serious risks to offering an opinion. Sense of unity gets replaced with conflicts of interest, personal needs that go unaddressed, hidden agendas, and a lack of coordination/communication. Lastly, joint progress is subverted by dropped balls, lack of feedback, and discontinuities in handoffs. Yet all of these problems are readily avoided through deliberate selection of the team and its goals and purpose (collective ambition) and paying careful attention to the prerequisites of team flow.

There is much to gained from discovering what is keeping your team members from experiencing flow while performing their tasks in service to the team. It is best not to dwell too much on the feelings of frustration these obstacles provoke. Try instead to focus everyone's attention on what they can do to promote flow. Knowing what to do empowers people to change. Of course, sometimes people refuse to face their shortcomings. In those cases, a dollop of negativity may be needed to drive the point home. (Frederickson, 2010).

As we noted in the write-up of the 2017 study, we consider the following principles helpful to get things going effectively:

- We participate because contributing to the team's collective ambition delivers enjoyment and/or meaning.
- We commit ourselves to challenging team goals that contribute to the collective ambition.
- We agree on clear personal goals that all align with a common team goal.
- We ensure that each team member utilizes his/her personal high skills in the team's interest.
- We communicate openly, and therefore supply each other with positive, direct, and constructive feedback/feedforward whenever possible.
- We create an environment where everybody feels safe to act, but allow acceptable risks that go together with challenging the goals that have been set.
- We make sure that everybody can focus on the task.
- We pay attention to each other in order to keep acting as a high-performance unit at all times.
- We collaborate from a foundation of mutual trust and respect.
- We challenge ourselves at all times to make progress.

Combining these principles with a strong collective ambition and solid team selection practices can give even a group of total strangers the opportunity to evolve into a team whose contribution can be far greater than the sum of its parts.

References

Amabile, T. M., Conti, R., Coon, H., Lazenby, J., & Herron, M. (1996). Assessing the work environment for creativity. *Academy of Management Journal, 39*(5), 1154–1184.

Amabile, T. M., & Kramer, S. J. (2011). *The progress principle: Using small wins to ignite joy, engagement, and creativity at work*. Boston, MA: Harvard Business Review Press.

Dattner, B., & Dahl, D. (2012). *The blame game: How the hidden rules of credit and blame determine our success or failure*. New York: Simon and Schuster.

Fredrickson, B. (2010). *Positivity*. London: Oneworld Publications.

Van den Hout, J. J. J., Gevers, J. M. P., Davis, O. C., & Weggeman, M. C. D. P. (2017). Overcoming impediments to team flow. *Challenging Organisations and Society, 6*(2), 1165–1181. https://www.cos-collective.com/cos-journal/2017-volume-6-issue-2/.

Wageman, R., Hackman, J. R., & Lehman, E. (2005). Team diagnostic survey development of an instrument. *The Journal of Applied Behavioral Science, 41*(4), 373–398. http://doi.org/10.1177/0021886305281984.

Chapter 6
Team Flow in an Organizational Context

This chapter goes into greater depth regarding team flow in an organizational context. First, we will discuss why teams are beneficial within organizations and why it is important to establish a collective ambition throughout the organization. After that we will provide an example of this principle by describing a healthcare organization which bases their whole organizational structure on self-managing teams.

6.1 The Importance of Uncovering Collective Ambitions Within Organizations

In Chap. 5 we saw that team members can experience many different impediments to experiencing flow while working on their personal tasks in the team's interest. Such impediments can arise from motivational, interpersonal, task-related, or environmental issues. Therefore, we state that on the unit level, organizational leaders and managers have a responsibility to create an optimal work environment for the units they supervise (e.g., departments, teams, work groups, etc.). It is important for each separate unit of the organization (including the organization as a whole) to clearly define the collective ambition and derive common goals. An organization can be defined as a group of people, most of whom have chosen to strive for a well-defined goal or ideal together, and all of whom have agreed to abide by certain agreements about their work and behavior in service of that goal or ideal (Weggeman, 2007). Within organizations, collective ambitions often arise in a natural way and result in common goals which contributing to this collective ambition. Earlier, we saw that a team's collective ambition is shaped by its members' reasons for collaborating, their values, their beliefs about how they should accomplish their goals, and their recognition of each other's complementary skills (van den Hout, Davis, & Weggeman, 2018). This collective ambition is thus

Jef J. J. van den Hout and O. C. Davis, *Team Flow*, SpringerBriefs in Well-Being and Quality of Life Research, https://doi.org/10.1007/978-3-030-27871-7_6

the starting point of team formation and the underlying reason everyone feels connected to the unit. Figure 6.1 shows the relationships between the organizational concepts of mission, vision, goal, and strategy, and how they define collective ambitions and policies for each unit.

The collective ambition is often the starting point of team formation or a re-energizer for putting everyone back into place and opening their minds to new and challenging team goals. These collective ambitions are the reason organizational members flock together in small teams (see below for a further explanation). It resembles what is really important for them, what they do well together, and what they are really trying to create together. A present and active collective ambition is the best recipe for establishing a climate that enables team flow experiences. Within an organization, the best way to have these collective ambitions and common goals form is by facilitating opportunities for people to connect and share motivations, values, beliefs, strengths, and ideas. From there, common and collective goals will emerge naturally. To create an ideal team flow environment within organizations, top-level organizational leaders should support an environment that facilitates the emergence of collective ambitions and common goals in the relevant units (often called project teams, task forces, or work groups). This means that these top-level leaders need to agree on collective ambitions and common goals and support them with necessary budgets, work hours, tools, space, and feedback. In this way,

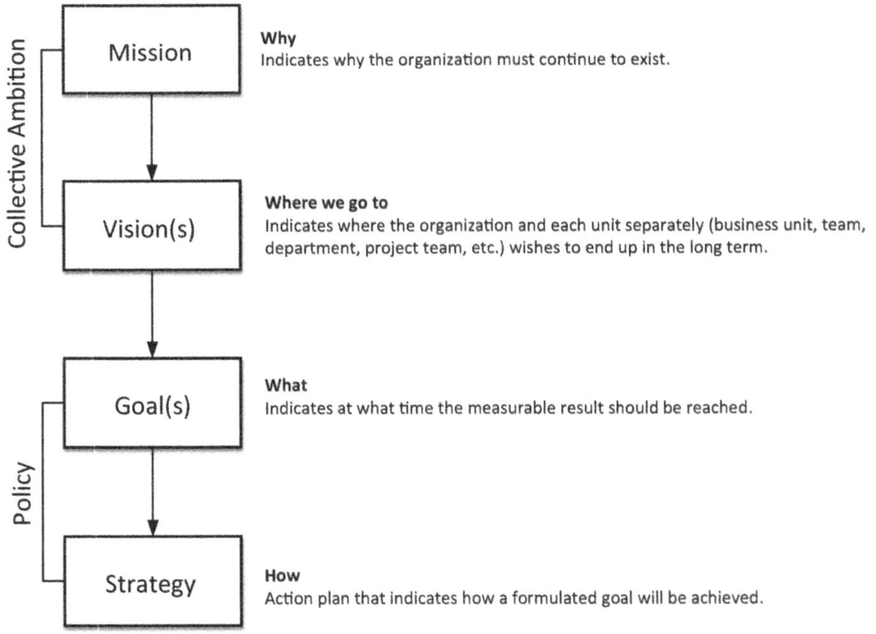

Fig. 6.1 Organizational concepts that define collective ambitions and policies (adapted from Weggeman, 2007)

bottom-up motivations will be fully aligned with the organization's mission and principles.

You could compare this natural way of teaming up around collective ambitions and common goals with the flocking behavior of starlings, which is controlled by three simple rules (Reynolds, 1987):

1. Separation—avoid crowding neighbors (short range repulsion), which means that starlings stay apart and avoid collisions with neighbors and repel each other at short distances.
2. Alignment—steer towards average heading of neighbors, which means that starlings stay in position and if any of their seven closest neighbors turn, they turn.
3. Cohesion—steer towards average position of neighbors (long range attraction), which means that starlings stay near each other and steer towards the center of the flock.

The rule of *separation* could be compared with an organizational member's need for professional autonomy. People appreciate their personal space and resent it when co-workers, and especially their bosses, intrude on that space. The rule for *alignment* could be compared with the collective ambition of a small group or team. People want to be part of something, contribute to something, and they love to witness the effect of their contributions directly (cf. small wins, Amabile and Kramer 2011; cf. immediate feedback, Csíkszentmihályi, 1990). These small wins are often created by small work groups or teams. The rule for *cohesion* could be compared with the mission of an organization as a whole. Each small team in a larger organization contributes to that organization's overall mission. In this way, each unit is part of and contributes meaningfully to a larger whole.

This metaphor of flocking starlings helps us understand the natural, instinctive, perhaps even automatic behavior of humans and teams within organizations. Leadership should refrain from imposing on its teams any policies or procedures that do not serve the creation of optimal cooperation both within and among teams (Barker, 1993; Hackman & Wageman, 2005; Lencioni, 2002; Peters & Pouw, 2004; Weggeman, 2007). Rather, they have to find the simplest possible way of stimulating and monitoring their organization's mission and vision. The importance of that simplicity is emphasized in the study performed by Lencioni (2002, p. 185): "As difficult as it is to build a cohesive team, it is not complicated. In fact, keeping it simple is critical, whether you run the executive staff at a multi-national company, a small department within a larger organization, or even if you are merely a member of a team that needs improvement." Organizations should also try to give their teams as much autonomy as possible in order to stimulate team flow. For instance, teams could coordinate their common goals with the organization's leadership and its other teams, possibly even seeking approval to ensure that the organization's overall efforts remain aligned. Our advice remains to keep it as simple as possible: It is vital to safeguard one's teams from excessive bureaucracy and not to bury them in rules and procedures as so many teams have been these past decades (Barker,

1993; Peters & Pouw, 2004; Weggeman, 2007; cf. Van den Hout, 2016). A team should be able to spend most of its time working towards the objectives that brought them together. If they cannot, their inevitable frustration will not just harm the team's effectiveness, but could demoralize the rest of the organization as well. Exactly how a team should achieve its goals is best left to the team in question, as they usually know best.

Autonomy is an important prerequisite for the achievement of team flow. As described by Csíkszentmihályi (1975, 1990, 1996), individual flow is characterized by, among other things, autotelic activity (doing things for the sake of doing them, intrinsic motivation) and a sense of control over one's own performance. This means that flow is more likely to occur when people are allowed to autonomously perform their personal tasks for the team. As such, in order for the team members to all experience flow together, which happens during an actual team flow experience, each individual team member will need to feel free to act autonomously in a way that is aligned with the team's objectives.

Based on our findings from the interview analyses and the answers to open questions on the Team Flow Monitor (see Chap. 7 for a description), we created a visual representation of the balance between finding alignment and providing autonomy in team cooperation (Fig. 6.2). When alignment is excessively discussed and monitored at the expense of autonomy, team members feel forced into involvement. Team cooperation starts to feel like a burden because it involves so much discussion, deliberation, and accounting. By contrast, if there is too much autonomy and not enough alignment in a team, it becomes a disorderly mess, with people pulling in all directions. It is still entirely possible for each member of such a team to experience individual flow, but the lack of coordination and cohesion puts team flow out of reach. The trick is finding the right balance between professional autonomy and alignment. Van den Hout (2016) showed that the way to do that is by establishing a collective ambition for the team and creating the prerequisites for team flow on that basis. Organization leaders must try to trust the collective ambitions that motivate each of their teams and give them free rein to realize those

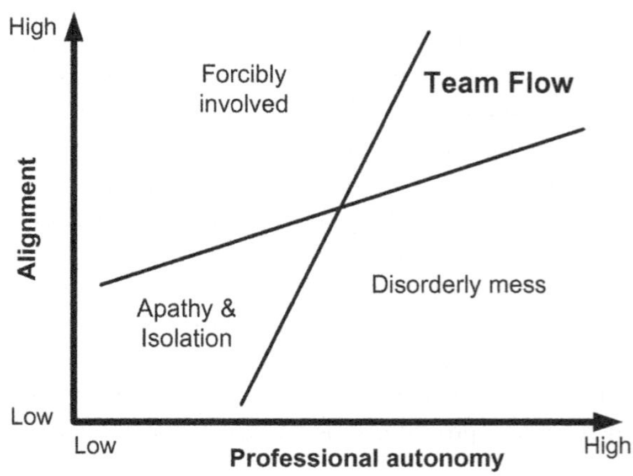

Fig. 6.2 The balance between professional autonomy and alignment (Van den Hout, 2016)

ambitions. All the leadership has to do is align the various collective ambitions in their teams to the organization's overarching mission and vision. The team flow model by Van den Hout (2016) is specifically designed for this purpose and helps organizations do this. The protocol teaches teams about the elements of team flow and helps them recognize, reflect upon, and realize those elements in their immediate environment. But, it is important for the team flow model and the protocol based on the Team Flow Monitor to be properly introduced by way of an inspiration session. Not doing so can cause the protocol to be viewed as pointless interference or even as a threat, even if the whole point was to safeguard the team's autonomy.

6.2 Buurtzorg Nederland as an Example of an Organization in Flow

One organization that, in the author's opinion, exemplifies support for and use of team flow is Buurtzorg Nederland. Buurtzorg Nederland provides home care with an innovative organizational structure and a compelling vision. Buurtzorg Nederland was born in 2006 out of growing dissatisfaction with the system in which home care was being offered in the region. Many policy measures within this sector have caused the sector as a whole to perform poorly and caregivers to experience steep declines in job satisfaction. Care was offered at very high prices and to an embarrassingly low standard. Buurtzorg Nederland used a fragmented approach for cure, care, and prevention, which resulted in many different caregivers having to visit the same patient. They tried to standardize their care, but that conflicted with the highly diverse and specific needs of their clients. The lack of time and high work pressure resulted in unhappy caretakers, with all its negative consequences. Most of these symptoms were clearly the result of "over-organization" in the Dutch home care sector.

Dissatisfied caregiver Jos de Blok and a few like-minded individuals founded Buurtzorg Nederland in response. Buurtzorg Nederland started with one self-organizing team in Almelo city with the goal of providing good care to clients. As of this writing (March 2019), Buurtzorg Nederland has grown to consist of 1050 self-organizing teams totaling 14,500 employees. From the start, the idea was to set up independent teams of 12 nurses working in neighborhoods of 5000–10,000 people. Today, Buurtzorg Nederland now spends fewer hours on patients than other home care institutions, and brought their annual revenue to over 410 million euros. Patient and employee satisfaction both skyrocketed, and they were awarded best employer of the year five times in a row. This recognition resulted in an additional 1200 employees each year. Their efficiency and independence reduced their overhead to 8% (sector average: 25%), which ensured they had more money available for their clients and innovation. Today, they are seen as a role model by the government and other care organizations, and organizations from different sectors all around the world now look to them for ideas.

In an interview a team member at Buurtzorg Nederland described her experience with the organization of Buurtzorg Nederland as follows:

> Employees are very happy with the amount of freedom they have. They aren't bothered by useless managers and bureaucracy. Buurtzorg Nederland is entirely organized around trust in the ability of its professionals. They are kept as free as possible of limiting rules and red tape. Our healthcare professionals are greatly appreciated by their patients and the organization. I've never worked in any organization that had this much positivity and energy.

This quote reflects all the performance indicators of Buurtzorg Nederland in a nutshell.

6.2.1 Buurtzorg Nederland: An Organization with a Mission

In their provision of care, Buurtzorg Nederland strives for better solutions for the clients that are sustainable and effective. Their chief ambition is for their clients to live happily in their own homes for as long as possible. This is the organization's mission and every team's primary purpose. According to Buurtzorg Nederland founder Jos de Blok, this is the starting point of every development process. To put it in his own words: "You need to start talking about the shared purpose or mission and from that start innovating the organization or way of working". The Buurtzorg Principles are very important to stay effective. Therefore, Jos expresses this vision often in meetings, inspiration days, events, etc.

6.2.2 The Self-Organizing Principle of Buurtzorg Nederland

Buurtzorg Nederland is convinced that self-managing teams can organize a lot together. The principles of self-management or self-managing teams are commonplace within Buurtzorg Nederland. Because they work with self-managing teams, they can connect better to the specific wishes and needs of the client. By creating care teams that include both nurses and non-medical assistants, they fully utilize their professionalism and problem-solving skills. Within Buurtzorg, they strive for maximum autonomy and minimal hierarchy, meaning the basis for their collaboration is trust. They aim to reduce complexity and when possible, they try to solve complexity with the use of information communication technology (ICT). All their caregivers consider themselves generalists, capable of caring for every type of patient. Their nurses are highly skilled professionals: 40% of them hold bachelor's degrees and each team has its own educational budget. To make optimal use of their capabilities, each team makes strong use of the clients' informal networks (e.g., neighbors, families) as they are more valuable than the formal organizational structures (Fig. 6.3).

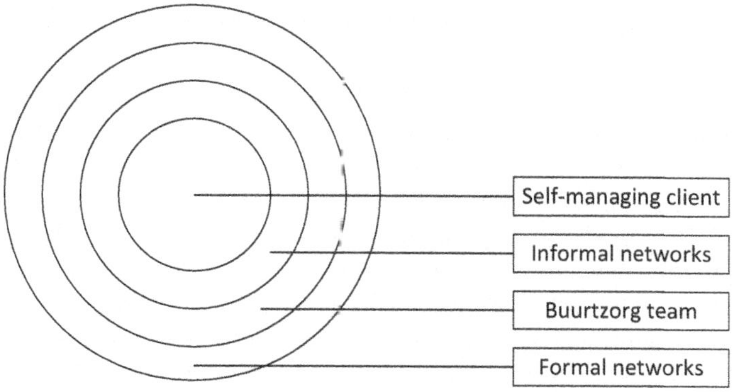

Fig. 6.3 Buurtzorg's model for Care (Buurtzorg Nederland, 2019)

Within their organization, Buurtzorg Nederland maintains three important guidelines. First, they recruit highly educated nurses and train their employees in collaboration skills, especially in solution-oriented work and communication. The team members are jointly responsible for care in their neighborhoods. Second, they have to make decisions in consensus, so that each team member feels responsible for the agreements made. Third and finally, all teams have to maintain a productivity level of 60%. If a team's productivity falls below 55%, the organization contacts them to ask how they can help bring them back up to the desired level.

A crucial underpinning of Buurtzorg Nederland's success is its lack of management team. There are only two directors, and they don't spend their time on management team meetings, strategic planning, and policy-making. When they feel the need to talk, they just do it face to face. In their eyes that works a lot more efficiently and applies to many issues that need to be picked up within the organization. As Jos de Blok said:

> The most optimal environment for our employees is one without bureaucracy. We try to be specific in why we are there so that our employees can focus on what they encounter. The context is guiding, and we do not distract our employees with too much top-down communication. Our whole organization is built upon trust, so trust is ensured. So, what we do is: If there is a problem that you have to solve, you can add something meaningful to it and then we get started. That's it!

The slogan at Buurtzorg Nederland is: "Keep it small! Keep it simple!" One sees that, for example, when a team requests more budget or additional support from staff. Coaches or the directors then ask questions to determine if this is really necessary, to find out if there are cheaper solutions or whether more people are needed. This lean, self-organization is the secret sauce that has employees loving their CEO, even though (or perhaps especially because) they can technically do without him. In this, Jos lives the vision of Buurtzorg.

6.2.3 Support for the Self-Organizing Teams

Year-round, teams can ask for help from the regional coach. Regional coaches help teams during their start-up phase and visit the team every two weeks. Once the teams are up and running, the coach will visit the team twice a year. The coaches have no position in the hierarchy, nor will they make any decisions. The sole purpose of the coach is to facilitate the teams in their work, identify team development opportunities, and report to the CEO so that he can further optimize the organizational framework. They safeguard the Buurtzorg vision and principles and mediate team conflicts. They focus not on the problem, but on which changes may be needed and how to ensure that the team is surrounded in positive energy.

6.2.4 How Buurtzorg Teams Organize Themselves

Buurtzorg works with small teams with 12 members or fewer, all (district) nurses and district healthcare providers who offer personal care and individual support to clients at home. The Buurtzorg teams are supported by a regional coach and a small national headquarters located in Almelo. There are no planners or managers working at Buurtzorg Nederland; all the teams have to manage themselves. Every neighborhood team is responsible and feels responsible for their own "company." Each team arranges its own planning, PR, hiring, etc. The sense of shared responsibility this engenders promotes intense commitment to the team.

Local teams at Buurtzorg Nederland are often adapted to the specific needs of their neighborhood, and they often need to be scrappy and entrepreneurial to build out a division that will meet the needs of regional stakeholders. Through this self-governing development, teams exemplify an important operational principle of ensuring that each team contributes to the organization's mission. This common purpose is paramount in every neighborhood team! The company credo "keep it small, keep it simple" also has its effect on the teams. Each team tries to get by with as few rules and regulations as possible, which promotes autonomy and job satisfaction.

The team as a whole is responsible for the client, though each client will have one or two team members who take point. In practice, that means no more than three or four different nurses will visit the client, allowing clients to build trust and familiarity with their caregivers.

To keep the team effective, most teams organize a team meeting every two weeks where they discuss all current issues (planning, vacations, education, team plan, reflections, progress, etc.). Team members are trained in organizing such meetings (with Solution Driven Communication, for instance), and in building consensus through the resolution of productive conflict, sometimes even using a disagree-and-commit model.

To further illustrate the collaboration within the Buurtzorg teams, we happily report on a specific Buurtzorg team that was asked how they experience collaborating together and how team flow emerges.

6.2.5 Buurtzorg Team De Beerzen in Team Flow

New Beginnings

'Setting up the office together, even that was great team-building.' These words, spoken by Ans van Hattum and recorded in the Brabants Dagblad of 4 June 2009, reveal how excited she was for her fresh start in a new and solid group of people. This group of nurses and caregivers from North Brabant were going to shake things up. They had been working for Zuidzorg, a large regional healthcare provider whose idea of daily in-home care was bureaucratic and impersonal. So, they joined Buurtzorg and set up shop for themselves in what had been a GP's office on the Kuijkseindseweg in Middelbeers.

Nine years later, the core of that team is still together, which is not at all surprising for a Buurtzorg team. This team emphasizes taking initiative, being considerate, and giving people the trust and autonomy to do whatever they think best at any given moment. At times, the team runs so well that their cooperation seems effortless.

We turn to a case study involving someone who switched into Buurtzorg from an outside company and how that experience is reflective of the team flow that is so common in the company.

The Job Interview

Six years of working at the nursing home in Bladel had been enough for Marjon. A friend told her about an interview with Jos de Blok she'd heard on the radio, and that's how she learned about Buurtzorg.

Marjon decided to call Buurtzorg and found herself talking to Danielle, who immediately invited Marjon for coffee…not at head office, but in Danielle's home. "I was taken aback. I'm calling a healthcare organization and the first thing they do is invite you to their home for coffee. Well, the whole thing was just, I was so surprised."

In the Buurtzorg team, nothing works the way she's used to. "After Danielle told me all about Buurtzorg, how they do things, I was buzzing with excitement. I'd have to drop by head office at some point, but I could go for an interview with the De Beerzen team right away. Or, well, it wasn't going to be a job interview, more of a chat over coffee, with as many team members there as possible."

That meeting turned out to be all or nothing. "They asked me some very real questions. The kind that matter. They weren't that interested in my qualifications, it was more about how I would deal with this situation or that. And, you know, self-reliance. You're out of time and a client is still in the bathroom. Do you step in and close their blouse for them? These are the things we talked about."

Marjon asked to work for 32 h. That would obviously have an enormous impact on the team. All of them would be working with her on a daily basis. So, they had her make a choice right there and then. Five days of ride-alongs, with five different coworkers. All in one week, as well, not spread out over a month. She would be able to get to know everyone without losing too much time. Marjon took a week of personal leave from the nursing home to discover how her prospective colleagues worked. "Each day was more exciting than the last. The way they worked, I was like Wow! This is what I want. This is what healthcare is supposed to be."

Job interviews at team De Beerzen are personal and based on trust. Applicants are immediately invited for coffee. One-on-one at someone's home first, then with the entire team. That doesn't mean everyone gets accepted—far from it! Marjon was grilled extensively on how she did her work and was expected to take a full week to get to know the team.

In the following week's team meeting, the team decided to hire Marjon. Unanimously, as the team requires. And Marjon? She hasn't looked back once since that first phone call with Danielle.

The Caregiver as Guest

Working in a nursing home as opposed to working for Buurtzorg, the difference is night and day as far as Marjon's concerned.

"I would watch this woman [in the nursing home] button up her own shirt for 5 min, thinking Do you really have this much time? Shouldn't you be on your way to the next one?"

The nursing homes she was familiar with had become so bureaucratic that her managers would dictate exactly how much care she was allowed to give and how many minutes she had before she was expected to move on to the next client. The whole reason Buurtzorg was created was to offer clients as rich and autonomous a life as possible, which means the client's wishes were taken very seriously.

"In the nursing home, people would just be washed every day. Head to toe. Whereas here, there's plenty of people, especially the older generation, who think one or two showers a week will do. Who are we to decide that they need to bathe every day?"

Marjon's statement contains much Buurtzorg wisdom. Here, the client comes first. The caregiver is a guest in their home. Caregiver and client decide together what care is needed and caregivers take the time to build meaningful relationships with their clients. Quality of life is the primary concern.

"They all have their own families, their own kids, their own problems, drama, illnesses, whatever. And now some outsider is showing up and that scares them. But here we are showing up…at their back door, and we say; "So, what would *you* like us to do for you today?" That may not seem like much, but it means the world to these people."

The Future for Buurtzorg De Beerzen

The members of team De Beerzen discuss the team's future in interview sessions they set up themselves. By talking to each other about their plans and desires, they learn what is on the horizon so they respond appropriately as a matter of course. At least, that was the belief and such has been the experience so far.

"Just sitting here with a cuppa," as they would say. "How are we doing with our hours, how is the care, how are we all doing at home, what do we think about expanding, what do we think about work, you name it."

To Each Their Own

Digital client registration was introduced a few years ago. The team now uses iPads for that purpose. Many of the colleagues are older and didn't grow up using these devices. It was lucky that Ans was spending more time at home when they were introduced. This gave her time to work it all out, especially because her kids could help her figure it out.

"Now all we have to do is call Ans, or drop by, to get help."

Lots of other tasks are divided up the same way."Scheduling. That's Danielle. She's been doing that all her life. The system we use to order supplies, Ellen knows all about that. And I do lots around the office—I manage things, organize things, order things."

On team De Beerzen, you do what you enjoy doing. Or what you're good at. Those are often the same thing anyway. As long as everyone is contributing, that's fine. If you don't want to preside over a meeting, you don't have to. And if you enjoy puzzling over the optimal schedule, then by all means keep puzzling.

"And if she ever gets tired of it, all she has to do is say so and I'll take a crack at doing the schedule."

A Safe Work Environment

Every team is made up of many personalities; Team De Beerzen is no different. You can tell by the fact that everyone enjoys different tasks, but there are plenty of other differences, too. For instance, when the team is very busy and new requests for care keep coming in (which has become increasingly common these past years), some want to say yes immediately while others would rather hold off.

The trick is to develop a sense for when things need to be discussed. It usually starts with a one-on-one discussion that is included in the next team briefing, but the team doesn't get involved unless people think it is necessary.

This open communication and preservation of people's individuality are characteristics of the safe work environment that team De Beerzen has created. They trust each other, and when something needs to be said, they do so swiftly and without fear of reprisal. This also makes them less afraid of professional failure. They stimulate each other to grow as a team.

"I think that's our team's strength. You don't need to know everything, but you always know what's going on."

Space for Flow

"I'm pretty focused on the BIS, the digital care plan. That has to be in place and, yeah, I like it done my way. I can be a bit of a tyrant about it, and one of my coworkers who doesn't really care about them has come to me and said [jokingly]: 'You make me feel like I can't do anything right.' And there are others who say they know how to do it or that they'll do it their own way, and we want to give everyone's approach a chance. But there still needs to be structure, you know, not ten different procedures."

The members of team De Beerzen listen to each other and give each other space, be it the space to be a stickler, or the space to improvise some order out of the chaos, like doing a quick client intake on the weekend just to "get things rolling" or filling in for an hour while a coworker takes her kid to daycare.

While everyone feels comfortable with the notion that everything works out somehow, there is actually a lot more going on. There are discussions about how to know when the team can take on a new client, and when it absolutely can't, forming clear guidelines about what to tell people who call in with requests for care, and making allowances for everyone's personal challenges. For an example of the latter, some team members are uncomfortable hooking up an IV drip or caring for a terminal patient, while others might struggle with the emotional burden of caregiving.

This mutual consideration requires respect for one another's autonomy. At De Beerzen, every team member gets the opportunity to do what they're good at, to be their authentic selves. This makes the most of everyone's abilities and allows everyone on the team to flourish.

Sometimes a team member needs to be slowed down a little. When their behavior impinges on a colleague's work, for instance. Or when a naturally hard-working team member takes on a little too much. It's important to address that before your coworker cracks under the strain. There's always someone willing to take on some of that load.

The trick is to develop a feel for these moments, both individually and as a team. Only then can the team members effectively challenge each other's very specific behaviors and discuss how those behaviors affect other team members and the performance of the entire team. This maintains team balance and cohesion and allows the team to stay in flow.

What Employees Say About Working at Buurtzorg Nederland

"The great thing about the team is that we share all responsibility between us, that we take the entire job on together and that we trust each other. Being part of this team just feels right."

"And it's great to manage ourselves. We don't *have* to do anything; We *get* to do things. You can follow your passion, take responsibility together. We can set our own goals for the team, like right now with providing complementary care, which we've included in our 12-month plan. Buurtzorg provides us the opportunity to grow."

"I can drop something into the WhatsApp group and be confident that it'll get handled. We can ask each other anything. You learn quickly in a team like that. We complete each other."

"Everyone accepts everyone else the way they are. You can be who you really are here. You're never walking on eggshells."

"We take an interest in each other, and we know an awful lot about each other, things like what's going on with work or at home, what aspects of work stress us out, anything like that. And the team is considerate of that. I think that's our team's source of strength."

Wrapping Up

In our wrap-up session with team De Beerzen, the team members listed a few more factors that helped them achieve team flow. For instance, they had this to say about client-focused care:

"We come into people's homes as guests to provide care in their natural environment. That allows us to provide meaningful care to our clients according to their wishes, and that's the beauty of it. Taking the time to sit and catch up with the client is so very important."

"When starting care, in those first two weeks, it's super important to discuss things with the client and the people around them (children, family, neighbors or friends). We get to know them, and they us, we learn what to look out for, and we discover what care they need, even if that care needs to come from outside the team. We're very good at that. That determines the quality of the care we provide and I love that. I would wish us on anyone."

6.3 Management Dogma as the Enemy of Team Flow

We would like to emphasize that a lot of flow within Buurtzorg Nederland is experienced during the execution of tasks while working together as a team. We were able to observe this during the many interviews and ride-alongs we did with Buurtzorg Nederland teams. Buurtzorg does not intentionally work in accordance with the team flow model or any other management model. But, after showing them our animation of the team flow model (https://www.youtube.com/watch?v=aoKCzn1-ZVk) a team member shouted: "Hey! That's us!"

The credo "keep it small, keep it simple" brings the human dimension into this organization and may be an important reason why team members at Buurtzorg Nederland experience [team] flow so easily. Many organizations today are over-organized, with very specific functions and too much vertical planning and control. As a result, organizations are becoming far too complex, which hinders the teams as they carry out their work. This results in frustration and a reduced sense of autonomy. Team flow, however, often occurs when team members are in a flatter [non-]hierarchy, feeding off each other's ideas and initiatives. When teams experience team flow, their members consider themselves equal. Their sense of autonomy is reinforced and people feel more appreciated. Buurtzorg Nederland's experience with team size also confirms that teams need to stay small (ideally no more than nine members) to stay workable (cf. Katzenbach & Smith, 1993), and that larger teams suffer significant impediments to effective cooperation (Amason & Sapienza, 1997; Haleblian & Finkelstein, 1993).

Within teams, the members themselves are responsible for the team flow climate. If they cannot work it out among themselves, they can call on the organization for assistance. The team remains responsible for aligning itself with its surroundings (i.e., other teams in the organization and the organization as a whole). The larger organization needs to facilitate and stimulate that process as much as possible.

Teams are mostly responsible for removing obstacles themselves, but when they cannot, they still need to be able to call on professional assistance from the central organization that can, for instance, respond by deploying a team coach. Support from the organization is clearly essential for teams to function well. Teams are often formed by the organization, but it would be even better for the teams to form themselves around a set of values, since that ensures optimal motivation. If that approach is chosen, the organization should take care to test whether the team's shared values (what we call collective ambition) matches the values (mission and vision) of the organization as a whole.

We can conclude that organizations need to provide those organizing themselves into teams with an inspiring mission and vision, clear and simple structure (rules), and on-demand support. The leadership, when extant on a team or empowering the high functioning of teams, becomes responsible for making it possible to create the prerequisites for team flow in each of the teams in their organization, ensuring that the collective ambitions of those teams are aligned with the larger organization's mission and vision.

6.4 Suggestions for Leaders Who Want to Work with Teams

The success of the team flow model lies in its simplicity. It is based on a core of positivity and that's why it works! The model has already proven itself in healthcare organizations, IT companies, research & development institutions, construction companies, and educational institutions. In order for teams to experience team flow, it is the responsibility of organization leaders to ensure the prerequisites for team flow are created in (and by) each team, and that the organizational structure, rules, and policies enable them to do so. They should therefore not bother the teams with too many unnecessary procedures, meetings and policies, but guide them towards the desired goal.

To conclude this chapter, we would like to give some tips for upper-level managers interested in creating flow-conducive environments for the teams in their organizations. Bear in mind these are tips for the leadership, not for team coaches:

- Ask each team for which you are responsible to set a collective ambition, possibly with a number of common goals. Then stand back and let them do their thing.
- Always judge a team by what the team as a whole delivers and never by individual contributions; the team will take care of that part internally.
- Appoint team coaches, not external leaders, managers, or coordinators. A coach facilitates the conditions for team flow, making him part of the team's support structure, not management.
- Enjoy and appreciate the beauty of a well-managed unmanaged team.

References

Amabile, T. M., & Kramer, S. J. (2011). *The progress principle: Using small wins to ignite joy, engagement, and creativity at work*. Boston, MA: Harvard Business Review Press.

Amason, A. C., & Sapienza, H. J. (1997). The effects of top management team size and interaction norms on cognitive and affective conflict. *Journal of Management, 23*(4), 495–516.

Barker, J. R. (1993). Tightening the iron cage: Concertive control in self-managing teams. *Administrative Science Quarterly, 38*(3), 408–437.

Buurtzorg International. (2019). Personal interviews with J. J. J. van den Hout, Jos de Blok, Gertje van Roessel, Nurses Marjon and Ria.

Csíkszentmihályi, M. (1975). *Beyond boredom and anxiety*. San Francisco, CA: Jossey-Bass Publishers.

Csíkszentmihályi, M. (1990). *Flow: The psychology of optimal experience*. New York: Harper and Row.

Csíkszentmihályi, M. (1996). *Creativity: Flow and the psychology of discovery and invention*. New York: HarperCollins.

Hackman, J. R., & Wageman, R. (2005). A theory of team coaching. *The Academy of Management Review, 30*(2), 269–287.

Haleblian, J., & Finkelstein, S. (1993). Top management team size, CEO dominance, and firm performance: The moderating roles of environmental turbulence and discretion. *Academy of management journal, 36*(4), 844–863.

Katzenbach, J. R., & Smith, D. K. (1993). The discipline of teams. *Harvard Business Review, 71*(2), 111–120.

Lencioni, P. M. (2002). *The five dysfunctions of a team*. San Fransisco: Jossey-Bass.

Peters, J., & Pouw, J. (2004). *Intensieve menshouderij*. Schiedam: Scriptum.

Reynolds, C. W. (1987). Flocks, herds and schools: A distributed behavioral model. *Computer Graphics, 21*(4), 25–34.

Van den Hout, J. J. J. (2016). *Team flow: From concept to application*. Dissertation, Eindhoven University of Technology, Eindhoven.

van den Hout, J. J., Davis, O. C., & Weggeman, M. C. (2018).The conceptualization of team flow. *The Journal of Psychology, 152*(6), 388–423.

Weggeman, M. C. D. P. (2007). *Leidinggeven aan professionals? Niet doen!*. Schiedam: Scriptum.

Chapter 7
Applications to Spark Team Flow

This chapter describes how organizations can foster a climate that promotes team flow. It goes into more detail regarding how team flow emerges and how the Team Flow Monitor (which is specifically designed to measure all elements of team flow) can be used as a helpful tool to measure the prerequisites and characteristics of team flow. By using this tool, teams can get an indication the efficacy of their current team dynamics and how organizations can intervene and guide their teams toward more team flow experiences.

7.1 Introduction

How can we help teams achieve team flow within professional organizations? Armed with the insight and information collected from the previous chapters, we will endeavor here to present two intertwined processes for promoting team flow experiences: a roadmap that was derived from a process theory on the emergence of team flow (as revealed by our results from Chap. 3), and an intervention protocol that builds on the Team Flow Monitor's usefulness as a diagnostic tool.

We know a lot about the factors that influence the effectiveness of teams at work in organizations, including group composition, cohesiveness, goal setting, and motivation. Researchers in this field have also investigated different kinds of teams and other forms of autonomous work groups that exist (Guzzo & Dickson, 1996; Hackman & Wageman, 2005; Katzenbach & Smith, 1993). But, the literature offers surprisingly little insight into the details of the circumstances and interventions that allow some organizations to make optimal use of their teams while others flounder.

When team members who are collaborating towards a common purpose encounter the subjective experience of flow together, the team, as a performing unit, improves its performance and, as a result, develops high collective competence

Jef J. J. van den Hout and O. C. Davis, *Team Flow*, SpringerBriefs in Well-Being and Quality of Life Research, https://doi.org/10.1007/978-3-030-27871-7_7

(Verhoeven, 2018). In Chap. 3 we introduced this team level concept as *team flow*, and defined it as "a shared experience of flow during the execution of interdependent personal tasks in the interest of the team, originating from an optimized team dynamic and typified by seven prerequisites and four characteristics". Based on an extensive literature review on flow and team dynamics, we suggest that team flow most aptly starts with establishing a collective ambition. From this collective ambition, the team readily sets the other six prerequisites for team flow, which are: a common goal, aligned personal goals, high skill integration, open communication, safety, and mutual commitment. Once in place, these prerequisites allow for the experience of the characteristics of team flow, which are: a sense of unity, a sense of joint progress, mutual trust, and holistic focus (as discussed in depth in Chap. 3).

We turn now to how the separate elements (prerequisites and characteristics) of team flow each arise and how they influence each other. To elaborate on this, we suggest that to enhance the occurrence of team flow experiences in an organizational context, the following two complementary strategies are necessary:

- Personal and team tasks should be designed so that the prerequisites for flow on the individual level and on the team level can be present and interrelated.
- Help people develop autotelic personalities by training them to recognize opportunities for collective action, honing their collaboration skills and setting bold-but-achievable (team) goals.

In combination, these two strategies contribute enormously to the occurrence of team flow experiences and the positive consequences of regular team flow experiences in work or business teams.

Figure 7.1 illustrates these two strategies. It shows that team members must develop both *team awareness* and *flow awareness*. With team awareness, team members have a better understanding of the team's current situation, meaning they are aware what each member of the team is doing, what they're good at, what they enjoy doing, and what's important to them. This team awareness should be combined with the understanding and experience of flow at both the individual and team levels. Team members who work together need to know which prerequisites need to be in place to develop (team) flow experiences. That allows everyone to foster (team) flow prerequisites for themselves, their teammates and the team as a whole.

This chapter goes into more depth on how the prerequisites and characteristics of team flow come into being. We build on existing team flow theory without making explicit assumptions about how it will be applied in different kinds of work teams. Whereas previous chapters have showed us unit-level examples of team flow, we will now describe how organizations can foster team flow. To that end, this chapter will answer the following two questions: "Through what processes does team flow emerge within professional organizations?" and "Which cultural aspects of organizations help teams to achieve team flow within professional organizations?"

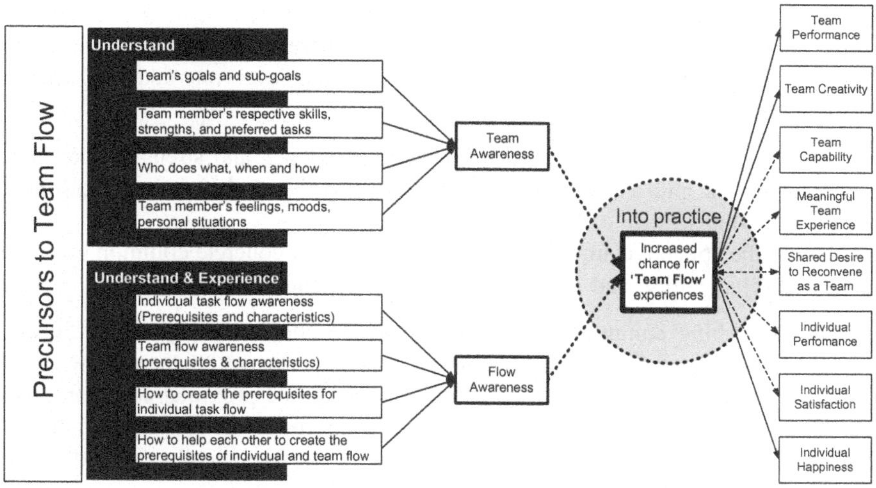

Fig. 7.1 Precursors to Team Flow

7.2 A Team Flow Roadmap

To help teams in organizations create an environment where team flow readily occurs, we put together a roadmap derived from our findings on the emergence of team flow and from existing theories on team development (e.g., Tuckman, 1965). This roadmap will help teams implement the seven prerequisites of team flow in four phases. Once the team has created these prerequisites together, they are far more likely to experience team flow and its concomitant benefits whenever they take action. The four phases are connect, construct, flow, and glow (Fig. 7.2).

7.2.1 Connect

In this phase, the team comes together to look for shared values and complementary skills. Many teams harbor opposing interests that can cause frequent conflict. But, if everyone acknowledges and shows appreciation for everyone else's interests as they look for values and goals they have in common and skills that can complement their own, that is the first step on the road to team flow. These shared goals, values, and complementary skills, once found, give rise to shared intrinsic motivation to cooperate in a specific activity. That shared intrinsic motivation for that specific

Fig. 7.2 The phases of maintaining a team flow climate

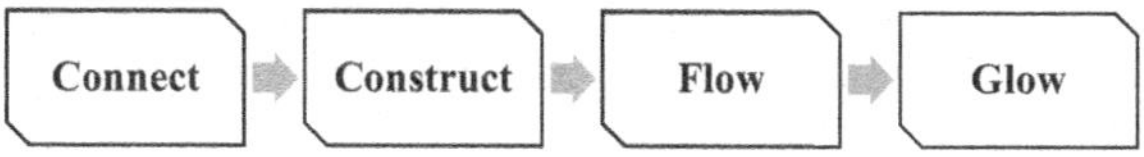

activity forms the foundation of the team's collective ambition. Based on its collective ambition, the team can start looking for a concrete common goal that would be challenging for them to achieve. The two vital steps everyone takes together in this phase are:

- Identifying the underlying motivations, shared values, and strengths that unite the members into a team and formulate a collective ambition based on those commonalities.
- Taking the collective ambition and aligning it with a concrete common goal that is both challenging and achievable within a reasonable timeframe.

An overarching common goal derived from a collective ambition is a useful guide and motivator for the team, but to foster experiences of team flow, more proximal common goals are needed as milestones. These proximal common goals are often derived either through planning or ad hoc from the long-term common goal and therefore closely aligned to it, but they are specifically tailored to the situation facing the team in the current moment, keeping team members engaged in the here-and-now and supporting experiences of both individual and team flow.

7.2.2 Construct

Phase 2 is where roles and tasks are distributed in a way that ensures all of the team members contribute based on their personal strengths and know exactly what they are expected to do. That means it is essential for proper task distribution that the team have both aligned personal goals and high skill integration. Everyone takes the following steps together in this phase:

- Setting a personal goal for each member of the team that is aligned to the common one—the personal goal should provide the team member with meaning, growth opportunities, and intrinsic motivation.
- Individuals derive their personal tasks, roles, and responsibilities from the team's common and personal goals, and then organize those personal items strategically so all team members are able to play to their respective unique strengths, thus bundling those strengths into a unified force (high skill integration).

It is also important for all team members to always be making progress together. For that to be possible, all team members must know exactly how they, as individuals, are doing, and how the team as a whole is doing. The team needs to be secure enough in its progress not to have to worry about its performance and about whether everyone is contributing as they should. When excessive risk is incurred due to a team member not performing a task correctly, prompt action is called for. It is important in the context of team cooperation, however, that team members be allowed to make mistakes and that mistakes, when they occur, be treated as growth opportunities for the individual and the team. Open communication and safety are obviously essential elements of that process. To that end, everyone should:

- Optimize mutual feedback on processes and outcomes so that everyone knows how they are doing and how the team as a whole is doing (open communication).
- Create an environment in which team members feel safe to act by eliminating unacceptable risks and supporting each other with positive and encouraging feedback (safety).

7.2.3 *Flow*

With the first six of the seven prerequisites for team flow in place, the time has come for action. The team can now start to work towards its common goal. It is important for everyone to stay on task, honor whatever agreements were made (or openly discuss any necessary changes and obtain consensus), and maintain the prerequisites for team flow. That requires mutual commitment. The team is now gradually approaching an actual team flow experience. Once that happens, the experience will grow more and more intense until someone or something in the team's environment pulls everyone out of the moment. The two vital steps everyone takes together in this phase are:

- Holding each other accountable for maintaining the requisite dedication and vigor for achieving personal goals and keeping each other on track by coaching each other on the task(s) (constructive feedback) and working to maintain the prerequisites of team flow (mutual commitment).
- Allowing team members to function autonomously and sharing experiences of unity, trust, focus, and progress that may transcend into experiences like team flow.

7.2.4 *Glow*

The moment of team flow has come and gone, and perhaps work has continued for a while. The team members and the people observing them won't soon forget their team flow experience. Everyone is basking in the afterglow. They'll certainly want to experience more team flow together, perhaps even with new people in a new team configuration. That means they will want to tackle similar challenges or even more ambitious ones. So, an important step they must take together is:

- Evaluating, reflecting, and enjoying the experience of team flow and agreeing to pursue new, challenging team goals.

We hope that the roadmap here described will help teams experience team flow together. It is especially well-suited to newly formed teams, but existing teams can certainly benefit from it. Bear in mind that many existing teams will have many of the prerequisites for team flow in place already and may have experienced team flow before (but it can be helpful for them to formally lay out these prerequisites). What many teams in a business environment often lack, however, is a climate that is conducive to team flow. To help existing teams experience more team flow together, we have created an intervention protocol. The team flow roadmap is just one part of that protocol, and we move now to the next ace in the hole: the Team Flow Monitor.

7.3 The Team Flow Monitor

To move the study of team flow experiences forward, researchers in the field need an instrument that can assess team flow experiences in business teams. In the following paragraphs, we introduce the Team Flow Monitor, which we developed in order to measure team flow and examine its relationship with individual and team-level work outcomes. To improve the presence of the elements of team flow in practice, the team must first gain insight into its current functioning, which the Team Flow Monitor allows them to do.

The Team Flow Monitor (TFM) is included in the appendix. The TFM contains 38 closed questions for respondents to rate on a scale from 1 ("strongly disagree") to 7 ("strongly agree") how noticeably present the eleven elements of team flow are. We report the mean team score for each of the eleven team flow elements, and also calculate three composite scores: one for the seven prerequisites (TFP), one for the four characteristics (TFC) and one as a total score for team flow (TFT). If you'd prefer a shorter questionnaire, we also have a Team Flow Quick Scan. The Quick Scan only contains one item for each team flow element, rather than 3 or 4 (NB: it is not as accurate, but is good for a very quick glance).

We also assess *team positivity* by asking team members to rate the ratio of negative statements to positive statements expressed in their team. Respondents answer on a scale ranging from 1 ('very negative') to 7 ('very positive'). Scores are aggregated to the team level by calculating the average score of all the members in the team. Higher scores on this variable indicate that team members experienced more positivity than negativity in the team. Next, we ask respondents to answer two questions regarding happiness: "How happy are you today?" and "How happy have you felt in the past month?"—respondents answer these questions on a scale from 1 ('low happiness') to 10 ('high happiness'). The percentage of time in task flow is assessed with a single item in which we ask team members to indicate the percentage of time that they personally experienced flow while working on their tasks for the team. To answer this question, respondents need to know what individual flow is. Therefore, we provide them with a definition of the task flow experience.

To provide a more qualitative understanding of the obstacles that undermine team flow, influences that could foster team flow and examples of team flow experiences in the mind of the team members, four open questions are included in the TFM. The first two questions ask under which conditions the team members are able (or unable) to experience flow in a work context. The third question asks the team members for suggestions on how to increase the amount of flow in their team. The final open question asks whether the team members can describe a specific instance of flow within the team.

Performance measures: To find out if teams are actually improving, it is important to record performance indicators relevant to the specific case at the beginning of a team flow intervention. Examples of such performance indicators are innovation, efficacy, efficiency, achieving deadlines, quality of work, etc. Objectively measurable indicators are preferable as they allow for valid comparisons when the questions are asked again later. If no such indicators are available, the next best option is self-reporting.

7.4 Intervention Protocol to Spark Team Flow

To spark team flow in organizations, Van den Hout (2016) designed an intervention protocol (Fig. 7.3) that will guide teams towards more team flow experiences. The protocol includes the Team Flow Model, which should help team members understand how team flow emerges through its elements (prerequisites and characteristics); the roadmap, which should help team members understand the order in which the team flow prerequisites are most easily created; and an illustration of the cyclical process by which teams can work to create the prerequisites for team flow,

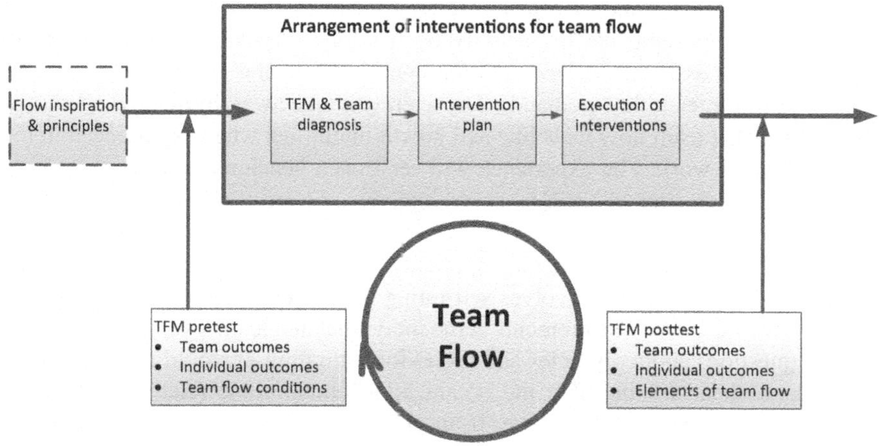

Fig. 7.3 Intervention protocol for sparking team flow in organizations

independently or with a team coach, guided by the results of the Team Flow Monitor.

When initiating the intervention protocol, a new team coach starts by meeting the people in the organization, usually the business leaders, and some, if not all, of the team members. That is a first step towards familiarizing themselves with the team's current situation and responsibilities. The next step is reading any relevant documents and interviewing the business leaders, the team leader (if there is one), and a few team members. Based on those conversations, the team coach will decide whether to start with a Team Flow Monitor pre-test or conduct a team flow inspiration session first. A clear benefit of the latter approach is that the team will be more willing take part in the measurement. It also provides the team coach with an opportunity to explain the TFM's purpose, which is to assist the team in creating a team flow climate. The downside of conducting a measurement after the inspiration session is that it may contaminate the results. It is imperative that, if you conduct an inspiration session before that first measurement, you explain to the team that the results are neither good nor bad, but merely a reflection of the team's current situation. The measurement is only effective if everyone involved answers the questions as honestly as possible. Only then will the results offer useful information for building a team flow climate.

During an *inspiration session*, the team coach introduces the team to flow and team flow theory. The participants will learn about all the elements of flow and team flow, as well as which of those elements they can deliberately create together. That makes team flow seem much more real. People are inspired to strive for flow and team flow by watching snippets of video, hearing quotations from interviews, and chatting about these examples of flow in the group. These sessions usually conclude with a team flow experience for which the person giving the workshop creates a team flow climate that lasts for the duration of a shared activity. What kind of activity that should be is determined with the team. Past activities have included playing Brazilian percussion instruments, cookery workshops, physical team sports activities (like for instance a fun ball tossing exercise), and business games (not online). It is important that the activity be fun for everyone and that each team member can be assigned a challenge that contributes to the greater whole (as the prerequisites for team flow demand). The team will take away from the workshop a fair idea of what team flow feels like and how it might feel when experienced in the context of their work. The experience will serve as a benchmark in their efforts to create the prerequisites of team flow and experience team flow at work.

The *measurement* with the Team Flow Monitor should take place at least a week after the inspiration session. That is important to give everyone a chance to get back to their routines. The TFM involves self-rating on all the elements of team flow as well as some outcome measurements at the individual and team levels and a number of open questions about obstacles and levers for team flow. It would also be wise to recommend ahead of time that the organization obtain some relatively objective measure of the team's performance. If an objective measure isn't available, triangulate subjective measures from multiple sources/perspectives.

The *diagnosis session*, the second team session after the inspiration session, is where the results are discussed. That discussion should take place with the participants seated in a circle without any tables between them—the proximity and lack of barriers facilitates the closeness of the team (literally!) and makes it clear that everyone is together in interpreting the results and finding ways improving. Take, for example, a team that achieves low average scores on open communication and mutual trust, but scores very highly on collective ambition and common goal. What they need to discover is how that happened and what can be done to fix it. There is often little point in trying to discover why a team scored poorly on a characteristic of team flow, since that is usually caused by low scores on one or more of the prerequisites for team flow. So, when a team scores poorly on open communication and mutual trust, the thing to do is look for ways to make communication in the team more open, constructive, and/or direct, depending on what the team decides is the specific problem with their communication (be aware that it might be something less visible like politics). Chances are that when the prerequisite of open communication is reinforced, the team will experience more mutual trust as well.

The team then has an open group discussion in which they diagnose their problems and look for interventions that will create a better team flow climate. One guide to help them determine which interventions are right for them is the previously introduced roadmap for team flow. When multiple prerequisites are partially or entirely absent, it matters which one you address first. There is usually no point trying to decide a common goal when the collective ambition has not been clearly established, for example. To come up with interventions, it may be helpful to split the team up into smaller groups for brainstorming, and then to discuss the ideas from these groups in the larger circle before agreeing on and finalizing an intervention plan together. Some examples of interventions are: goal sessions to determine common and individual goals, carousel presentations telling your teammates about who you are and how you'd like to contribute to the team, daily stand-ups to keep each other apprised of everyone's progress, monthly happy hours during which people share stories about flow experiences, celebrations of the team's successes, celebrations of its failures and the lessons learned, or any expression or ritual that conveys what the team stands for, like a song, poem, lip dub, or animation.

Based on which interventions were selected and included in the intervention plan, the team decides when another TFM measurement should be performed. That second measurement, the *post-test*, is used to evaluate the effect the interventions have had and whether further and/or different interventions are required. If there are, the team goes through another cycle of the process, and they will continue to do so until the team feels no further interventions or TFM measurements are needed.

The intervention protocol was created using the design-based research approach. By means of this approach, which uses existing theory, case-based evidence, and real-world experience to help solve problems in the field (van Aken, 2004; Collins, Joseph, & Bielaczyc, 2004; Romme, 2003), we determined which interventions work more and less effectively to foster team flow. The real-world problem we tried

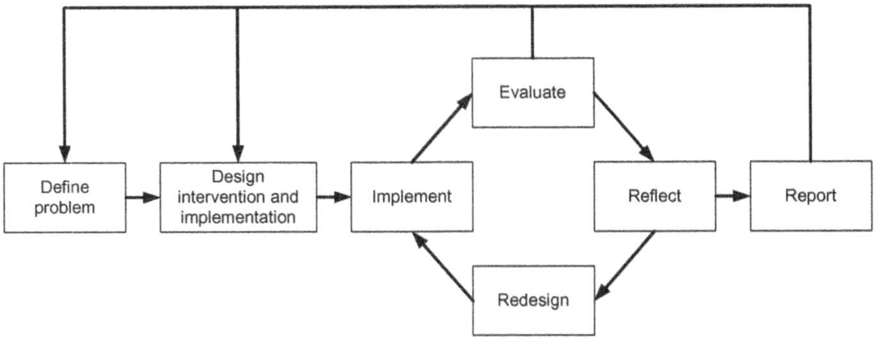

Fig. 7.4 The design-based research process (Ropes, 2010)

to solve in our research is how best to stimulate team flow in a given organizational environment. The solution involves the prerequisites of team flow and a set of interventions that help create these team flow prerequisites for a team, thereby making it more likely that the team and its members will experience team flow (more frequently and/or intensely). With this method, interventions can be tested using a quasi-experimental design (Cook, 1979). Once a draft solution for an intervention in a specific context has been tested, the results are analyzed and used to improve the design. Then the cycle starts again (Fig. 7.4). We encourage researchers and coaches to use the intervention protocol to define the 'problem' and to design and test specific interventions that could spark the presence of [any of] the elements of team flow.

Coaching teams towards more team flow experiences can be done using a process model that follows the emergence of team flow as described in Chap. 3. Such a step-by-step plan can help teams work together to realize the elements of team flow. Using the Team Flow Monitor in combination with the intervention protocol, teams can gauge whether the climate is optimally conducive to team flow and, if it is not, determine what can be done to improve it. The interventions teams perform are then monitored and their effects measured. This approach was created based on the interviews with team members and team experts, then tested and approved in the cross-case-study research (Van den Hout, 2016). The respondents who evaluated the study indicated that they found it both useful and desirable; taking part in this research has been very productive for all of them.

References

Collins, A., Joseph, D., & Bielaczyc, K. (2004). Design research: Theoretical and methodological issues. *Journal of the Learning Sciences, 13*(1), 15–42.

Cook, T. D. (1979). *Quasi-experimentation: Design & analysis issues for field settings*. Boston: Houghton Mifflin.

Guzzo, R. A., & Dickson, M. W. (1996). Teams in organizations: Recent research on performance and effectiveness. *Annual Review of Psychology, 47*(1), 307–338.

Hackman, J. R., & Wageman, R. (2005). A theory of team coaching. *The Academy of Management Review, 30*(2), 269–287.

Katzenbach, J. R., & Smith, D. K. (1993). The discipline of teams. *Harvard Business Review, 71*(2), 111–120.

Romme, A. G. L. (2003). Making a difference: Organization as design. *Organization Science, 14*(5), 558–573.

Ropes, D. C. (2010). *Organizing professional communities of practice*. Doctoral Dissertation. University of Amsterdam. Retrieved from http://dare.uva.nl/record/1/337261.

Tuckman, B. W. (1965). Developmental sequence in small groups. *Psychological Bulletin, 63*(6), 384–399.

van Aken, J. E. (2004). Management research based on the paradigm of the design sciences: The quest for field-tested and grounded technological rules. *Journal of Management Studies, 41*(2), 219–246.

Van den Hout, J.J.J. (2016). *Team flow: From concept to application*. Dissertation. Eindhoven: Eindhoven University of Technology.

Verhoeven, B. (2018) *Let's flow! Transformational leadership and team effectiveness: The mediating role of team flow in organizations*. Master Thesis. Eindhoven: Eindhoven University of Technology.

Chapter 8
Discussion

After describing the concept of team flow, potential impediments to team flow, examples of team flow experiences in the workplace, and the process of how companies can guide their teams towards experiencing more team flow, we will conclude with some general observations and new ideas on flow and team flow, and how this field of research might develop in the coming years.

8.1 Conclusions

We've seen that people enter flow when they focus completely on the proximal goals of the activity they are currently engaged in, closing themselves off to stimuli unrelated to the task at hand. Constant, immediate feedback on those proximal goals during execution of the task is what sustains the flow experience. The individual focuses on the task, and observes the progress being made, which increases focus and improves performance, which in turn ensures more progress, etc.

It is usually a pleasurable and satisfying experience, often creating a powerful desire to continue performing the activity in question. The experience is always temporary, but it is possible to find oneself in a process that ignites a series of flow experiences as the actor performs each of the tasks related to that process.

Flow experiences vary in intensity from one experience to the next. Their intensity can even fluctuate over the course of a single experience until it fades entirely. There are always residual effects, though, such as satisfaction, increased self-confidence, and a better sense of one's own abilities. These residual effects generate a desire to engage in that activity again, seeking out new challenges in an effort to have more flow experiences. The same goes for teams. A soccer team in a 'winning mood' can experience team flow for the duration of an entire match. With the right state of mind, they can even experience long periods of team flow in a series of consecutive matches.

Jef J. J. van den Hout and O. C. Davis, *Team Flow*, SpringerBriefs in Well-Being and Quality of Life Research, https://doi.org/10.1007/978-3-030-27871-7_8

Team flow is a phenomenon in which a group of people working on the same activity lose themselves in that activity, focus on it completely, and close themselves off to stimuli unrelated to the task at hand. In team flow, team members experience their own individual task flow *as well as* that of the other team members. The individual's tasks and those of the teammates are mutually dependent, creating a strong web of connections whose complexity determines the team dynamic and from which one is able to derive a flow experience.

Although individual task flow experiences are happening for each team member as they perform their interdependent tasks, the way their tasks and experiences intertwine makes the shared experience unique, which is why team flow has unique characteristics. The paradox of the team flow experience is that even as the team members perform interdependent tasks, they each remain autonomous in their performance of those tasks, though they must still coordinate with the rest of the team. This makes it possible to experience both individual task flow and then experience team flow on top of that, which adds the four unique characteristics of team flow to the experience (sense of unity, joint progress, mutual trust and holistic focus). These characteristics and the seven prerequisites of team flow (collective ambition, clear challenging common goal, aligned proximal personal goals, high skill integration, open communication, safety and mutual commitment) are what distinguish team flow from individual flow.

Teams can be tightly knit or loosely coupled. A crew of four rowers needs to be tightly knit: the team members work in close physical proximity and are constantly aware of each other's performance. When those performances align and amplify each other, the team can experience team flow together. This type of team flow can be disrupted by even a single team member missing a stroke. The team will immediately lose its collaborative flow until they can work out what happened, realign their efforts, and allow team flow to re-establish itself. For team flow to occur in a tightly knit team, every member of the team needs to be experiencing some level of individual flow in the tasks they are performing for the team. If one team member drops out of the flow experience, so will the others. By contrast, short track bicycle relay races have loosely coupled teams. In a relay team, members perform one after the other and the team's result is simply the sum of all individual results. Any one team member's individual performance cannot directly influence every other team member's performance to the same extent we see in rowing.

Teams in organizations are usually of the loosely coupled variety, though tightly knit ones exist as well (like surgical teams fighting for a patient's life in the OR). Most members of most teams in organizations aren't constantly aware of what the other members of their team are doing from moment to moment. For example, members of the Buurtzorg team each visit their clients by themselves. These kinds of teams only meet occasionally to discuss things like scheduling, task distribution, and long-term objectives. Shared and simultaneous experiences of team flow are less common in teams like this. Because the 7 prerequisites of team flow are still in place, the members of these teams are more likely than most to experience individual task flow and it would make sense to call that team flow, since they are still performing their tasks in service to the team and their individual task performance still influences the other team members. As such, team members are still feeling like their actions are coordinated and synergistic; it's just not happening simultaneously. One could still use tools like the Team Flow Monitor and the Team Flow Quick Scan to evaluate the collaboration of these teams. For scientific studies, though, it is important to carefully describe the type of collaborative activity being undertaken and to add questions to the Team Flow Monitor to determine, for instance, whether team members experienced flow *at the same time as, in close proximity to,* and/or *while interacting with* the other team members. Questions like these allow for a more precise understanding of team flow during various collaborative activities.

In general, team flow experiences for loosely coupled teams in organizations don't require equal participation or contribution. Because the links within the team are more flexible, it is not as much of a problem when some team members have a less intense team flow experience than others, provided they don't actively obstruct team flow.

It is important for teams in organizations to alternate between flow and non-flow. The team needs to take the time to reflect on their goals and actions or risk getting stuck in a rut, which will erode team effectiveness over time. Occasional differences of opinion, even conflict, can be helpful in breaking out of 'group think' and re-evaluating priorities, but also tend to exist outside of flow. When teams and their members take time to reflect on their personal and collective actions, it is impossible, by definition, for the team or individuals to be in flow, since individuals experiencing flow are not self-aware.

Organizational leaders are likely to be very interested in the benefits of team flow, the results of the team experiencing team flow, and even the results of teams whose work depends on that of the team experiencing flow.

You could ask members of a team to indicate, at regular intervals, how often they experienced flow over a given period, say two weeks or a month. If you do, it would make sense to also test for the presence of the prerequisites and characteristics of both flow and team flow. Having team members evaluate the degree to which each of these elements was present will give you some idea of where to intervene to improve the team flow climate and the odds that the team will experience (more) team flow. To that end, we have developed and tested two tools: the very thorough Team Flow Monitor and the more streamlined Team Flow Quick Scan (both available from our website: goteamflow.com). Both generate reports with suggestions for interventions to improve the team flow climate based on the presence (or absence) of the elements of team flow. It is a sensible precaution to have teams perform one or both regularly in order to sustain the optimum team flow climate. Teams working in such a climate are likely to perform better, find their work more satisfying and, in the end, are happier overall.

8.2 Future Research

The proposed conception of team flow by van den Hout, Davis, and Weggeman (2018) raises a number of important questions that future research will need to address. The first is a comparison of holistic and concatenative conceptions of team flow. For instance, even though Sawyer states that it is possible for a group to experience flow at a holistic level even as some individuals do not have an individual flow experience (Sawyer, 2003, 2007), we contend that it is unlikely, and that for team flow to occur all individuals have to be in flow. But, what happens when only parts of the team experience individual flow—which type of flow is that? Similarly, what happens if most of the team is deriving flow from the team dynamic, but not everyone is, and there is no team-level experience—does that still constitute team flow? In response to those concerns, we posit the existence of both *partial team flow*, which occurs when only some members of the team experience flow as a function of the team dynamic, and *full team flow*, which is when the entire team is experiencing flow as a function of the team dynamic. Future research will need to ascertain empirically whether having every member of the team deriving a flow experience from the team dynamic necessarily yields a team-level experience.

Future research could also examine whether the construct of team flow as defined and described in this book is as useful to artistic and sports groups as it is to professional teams and whether it is more or less useful in that context than Sawyer's conceptualization of group flow (e.g., Sawyer, 2007).

Another interesting aspect of flow is that individual flow experiences can range from microflow to deep flow. Microflow experiences are often simpler activities that serve as pockets of positivity that can be accessed on a limited basis, and reflect the lower end of the flow continuum with some of the characteristics of flow being compromised (Csíkszentmihályi, 1975; Davis, 2010). Deep-flow experiences, by contrast, are full-fledged flow experiences produced by complex, structured activities. Elaborating on this distinction, whether an individual team member experiences microflow or deep flow depends upon the effort they must expend to fulfill their personal task. It is important for team members' individual flow experiences to maintain or improve the team's harmony (the sense of unity), maintain or improve its position (contributing to the sense of joint progress), and maintain (i.e., not disrupt) shared focus and trust. For instance, individual flow could be disruptive when someone is striving too hard to optimize their personal performance (too much ego) without taking into account the team's overall performance. Take for example that one striker on the team who takes impossible shots on goal in a bid for glory while ignoring teammates who are in a better position to score. This person may experience individual flow, but is detracting from the team dynamic and is therefore inhibiting the experience of team flow for everyone on the team. So, the execution of a team member's personal tasks needs to support the team dynamic in order to promote an experience of team flow.

Team flow, then, is what happens when all members of a team experience flow (be it micro or deep) that originates from a team dynamic and where its members share in feelings of harmony and power. Consequently, team flow can differ in its intensity depending on the degree to which the elements of team flow are present. In this book, team flow is defined as a shared experience of flow during the execution of interdependent personal tasks in the interest of the team, originating from an optimized team dynamic and typified by seven prerequisites and four characteristics.

On a similar note, future studies should consider whether there is a 'tipping point' at which a certain amount of partial team flow creates the conditions required for team flow to emerge around the remaining members of the team. There is also the question of how experiencing flow from the team dynamic occurs in people, and how it spreads to become team flow. Is there a contagion effect within teams, such that flow starts in just one or two people and infects the others, or does it emerge for everyone (or a majority) simultaneously? For example, Bakker (2005) shows that the more often music teachers experience flow, the more likely their students are to experience an episode of flow as well. Likewise, according to Engeser and Schiepe-Tiska (2012), the more individuals are interacting, the greater this contagion effect. A further complication is the fact that the characteristics of the flow experience interact in a non-linear way (Ceja & Navarro, 2011), and no study to date has analyzed all of the characteristics using non-linear models. Thus, there is a great deal of research still to be conducted on this question.

This book extends the body of knowledge on flow, interpersonal flow, and especially team flow with insight into its occurrence in business organizations. Moreover, we have gained a better understanding of individual flow and team flow and how the two concepts relate. This book gives insight into the conceptualization of team flow and shows how it can be measured using self-rating scales. Finally, the book suggests ways to build high-performance teams and draws a roadmap for how to spark team flow within teams and organizations.

The Team Flow Model, a simplified, diagrammatic representation intended to help team members learn and understand how team flow emerges, is inherently limited in the sense that it is perfectly possible for relationships unmarked in the model, possibly involving concepts entirely absent from the model, to affect whether or not team flow is experienced. The sacrifices to clarity and usability required to construct any model at all mean that real-world experiences can diverge from the model. Future studies of the relationships among the elements of team flow could subject the model to additional tests, confirming its effectiveness or finding ways to make it more accurately reflect reality.

All told, our theory and findings on this new concept of team flow open up many avenues for future research. Such research could involve more specific performance measures and more control variables (e.g., diversity, work context, compositions, tasks). It could study specific prerequisites for team flow in contexts other than work and ways of encouraging team flow in work environments traditionally considered unsuited to it. Studies could also be conducted that measure team flow experiences at various points during the collaboration process to investigate at what times in a collaboration team flow is most likely to emerge. It would similarly be very interesting to include in such studies measurements of the frequency and intensity with which team flow is experienced. In addition, the central element of our team flow model, the collective ambition, could set in motion a whole new area of organizational design research. Are the exemplifying quotations in this book indicative of a whole new field of organizational design research that will focus on teams' collective ambitions as a means of directing entire organizations? Can a well-chosen collective ambition relieve the tension between team alignment and individual autonomy? How, theoretically, could a tool be designed that helps organizations in various contexts make the most of its teams and their collective ambitions?

8.3 Closing Comments

It is important for people to care about what they are doing and decide for themselves the contexts in which they will apply their effort, attention, care and connection. As such, a key component of productivity in knowledge work is the creation of meaning (Wrzesniewski, Dutton, & Debebe, 2003). In teams, meaning has the potential to develop into an internalized *raison d'être* that can translate into a foundation for team flow. Consequently, employers should invest in developing and aligning collective, team, and personal ambitions for their organizations, and make sure that this alignment is a constant in the workplace. In fact, there are three main tasks business leaders should undertake to foster team flow: they should agree with team members on well-designed but challenging team tasks, they should support well-composed teams upon request; and they should be clear about the overarching values and value proposition of the organization.

A carefully thought-out collective ambition ranks foremost among the prerequisites for team flow. Its presence can be encouraged through guidelines and interventions and fosters the kind of environment (team dynamic) in which teams (frequently) experience team flow together. When attempting to foster more team flow experiences in a business environment, it is useful to consider which of the prerequisites of team flow is most readily created by the team members or their employer. To help people experience more flow, it is not enough to create an environment that is conducive to flow, but also to teach people to be aware of the elements that make team flow more likely to emerge.

Well-being at work (and outside of work) is not the automatic result of adding together a series of flow experiences. The whole, in this case, is definitely more than the sum of its parts. One must respect the fact that there are personal and external factors, over which limited control can be exercised, that limit the emergence of team flow. As such, it is critical to remember that team flow *cannot* occur on demand—indeed, attempts to control or force it will backfire (cf. Csíkszentmihályi, 1997; Gardner, Csíkszentmihályi, & Damon, 2001). To lift the entirety of a team into a unified team flow experience, it helps to develop and reinforce a system of meaning and values that lend purpose to a team's existence.

This book not only clarifies the prerequisites and characteristics of team flow in a business context, it also suggests that shared experiences can affect both team performance and well-being—two variables that have long been of interest to organizational scholars. This opens numerous fascinating avenues for future research into ways to structure teamwork that improve not just how teams perform, but how their members feel about their collaborations. Such research may well benefit individual employees as well as their teams *and* the organizations in which those teams operate. Hopefully, this book will inspire scholars and practitioners alike to further investigate the outcomes of team flow and make the practice and experience more widespread.

References

Bakker, A. B. (2005). Flow among music teachers and their students: The crossover of peak experiences. *Journal of Vocational Behavior, 66*(1), 26–44.

Ceja, L., & Navarro, J. (2011). Dynamic patterns of flow in the workplace: Characterizing within-individual variability using a complexity science approach. *Journal of Organizational Behavior, 32*(4), 627–651.

Csíkszentmihályi, M. (1975). *Beyond boredom and anxiety*. San Francisco, CA: Jossey-Bass Publishers.

Csíkszentmihályi, M. (1997). *Finding flow: The psychology of engagement with everyday life*. New York: Basic Books.

Davis, O. C. (2010). *Defining microflow through the context of a waiting paradigm*. Dissertation: Claremont Graduate University.

Engeser, S., & Schiepe-Tiska, A. (2012). Historical lines and an overview of current research on flow. In S. Engeser (Ed.), *Advances in flow research* (pp. 1–22). New York: Springer.

Gardner, H. E., Csíkszentmihályi, M., & Damon, W. (2001). *Good work: When excellence and ethics meet*. New York: Basic Books.

Sawyer, R. K. (2003). *Group creativity: Music, theater, collaboration*. Mahwah, NJ: Lawrence Erlbaum Associates.

Sawyer, R. K. (2007). *Group genius: The creative power of collaboration*. New York: Basic Books.

van den Hout, J. J., Davis, O. C., & Weggeman, M. C. (2018). The conceptualization of team flow. *The Journal of Psychology, 152*(6), 388–423.

Wrzesniewski, A., Dutton, J. E., & Debebe, G. (2003). Interpersonal sensemaking and the meaning of work. *Research in Organizational Behavior, 25*, 93–135.

Appendix

See Tables 1 and 2.

Table 1 The Team Flow Monitor (TFM)

Team flow constructs	Cronbach's Alpha	Question items ("In the team in which I participate...")
Prerequisites of team flow		
Collective ambition The extent to which the same ambition is collectively shared (CA)	0.83	...we share the same ambition
		...we form a team from an inner drive to accomplish things together
		...we feel that engaging in the team process is intrinsically rewarding
Common goal A collective goal that is endorsed by everyone (CG)	0.80	...we endorse the established goals
		...we agree on clear goals
		...the shared goal offers a suitable challenge
Aligned personal goals The presence of personal goals that also contribute to the common goal (APG)	0.82	...we are stimulated to determine a personal goal
		...personal goals are derived from the common goal
		...personal goals are important to the team
		...personal goals are compatible with those of the team
High skill integration The arrangement of individual merits into a collective strength (HIS)	0.84	...every team member takes up a suitable challenge
		...we make use of each other's skills
		...individual skills are integrated to form a coherent whole skill

(continued)

Jef J. J. van den Hout and O. C. Davis, *Team Flow*, SpringerBriefs in Well-Being and Quality of Life Research, https://doi.org/10.1007/978-3-030-27871-7

Table 1 (continued)

Team flow constructs	Cronbach's Alpha	Question items ("In the team in which I participate…")
Open communication: Openness in communication with one another	0.88	…we receive feedback from one another that lets us move forward
		…we provide each other with feedback whenever we can
		…everyone receives clear feedback
Safety: The level of psychological safety needed to engage in action	0.92	…we each feel that it is safe to perform our tasks
		…there is a safe climate for learning
		…we each feel that it is safe to take risks
		…there is positive climate in which to perform
Mutual commitment: The level of commitment towards one another	0.84	…we pay attention to each other's activities
		…we know from one another who does what
		…we concentrate on smooth collaboration
Characteristics of team flow		
Sense of unity: The extent to which the team acts in unity	0.95	…we feel as one with the team
		…we are fully involved with the team
		…the team acts in unity
Sense of joint progress: A collective feeling of accomplishment	0.88	…we collectively make progress
		…I feel that we make joint progress
		…together we achieve more
		…actions naturally flow in quick succession
Mutual Trust: The level of mutual trust in the cooperation	0.91	…we have trust in each other to collectively complete our task
		…there is an atmosphere of trust among us
		…we, as a team, trust that we will be able to complete the task successfully
		…we have trust in each other to collectively complete our task
Holistic Focus: The extent to which everyone focuses on the common goal	0.86	…everyone is completely focused on the shared task
		…the team as a whole is in focus
		…everyone is fully focused on executing his/her task for the team

Note The use of (parts of) the Team Flow Monitor for any commercial purpose is expressly prohibited. The use of the Team Flow Monitor for scientific purposes is permitted if the collected data is shared with the author of this paper. The Dutch version of this survey is available from the author upon request

Table 2 Comparing the elements of five different conceptualizations of plural flow with individual flow

Team flow element	Related element(s) of…				
	Interpersonal flow[a]	Group flow[b]	Social flow[c]	Mosek's[d] team flow	Individual flow[e]
Collective ambition	Feeling a shared sense of identity Enjoyable and intrinsically rewarding		Emergent challenges are important and meaningful to the entire group Joy, elation and enthusiasm felt and shared throughout group performance The experience builds meaning and a collective sense of purpose The group desires to repeat the experience	Game plan Team autoteletic experiences Team optimal arousal	Intrinsic motivation
Common goal		The group's goal		Clear goals	Clear proximal goal(s)
Aligned personal goals				Clear goals	Clear proximal goal(s)
High skill integration		Blending egos Equal participation Familiarity	The collective competency of the group is sufficient to dispatch challenges Group members are uniformly highly competent	Team challenge-skill balance	Challenges matched to skill level
Open communication	Having his/her perspective broadened by the other person	Close listening Familiarity Communication	Group members have task-relevant knowledge and skills Task feedback is clear and immediate Task feedback is primarily cognitive and secondarily affective Social process feedback is primarily affective and secondarily cognitive Emotional communication during group work	Team unambiguous feedback Team communication Coaching style	Clear and immediate feedback

(continued)

Table 2 (continued)

Team flow element	Related element(s) of…				
	Interpersonal flow[a]	Group flow[b]	Social flow[c]	Mosek's[d] team flow	Individual flow[e]
Safety	Not worrying about what outsiders think	The potential for failure		No fear of failure/A sense of control	No fear of failure/A sense of control
Mutual commitment			Group members focus on each other as well as the task to receive feedback	Team concentration	Total concentration Oblivious to distraction
Sense of unity	Not feeling self-conscious with each other Feeling a shared sense of identity	Blending of egos	Shared intense absorption in and engagement with the task Less awareness of self Surrender of self to the group Emotional contagion within the group and observers outside the group	Merging of action and awareness	Loss of reflective self-consciousness
Sense of joint progress	Feeling able to respond almost instantly to presenting situations as a pair	Moving it forward		Merging of action and awareness	Merging of action and awareness
Mutual trust		Being in control		No fear of failure/A sense of control Team confidence	No fear of failure/A sense of control
Holistic focus	Total concentration on the shared activity Time passing differently than normal (faster or slower)	Complete concentration	Group members focus on each other as well as the task to receive feedback Shared intense absorption and engagement with the task High attention to group members or teammates Loss of sense of time	Time transformation	Distorted experience of time passing Complete concentration

(continued)

Table 2 (continued)

Team flow element	Related element(s) of…				
	Interpersonal flow[a]	Group flow[b]	Social flow[c]	Mosek's[d] team flow	Individual flow[e]
Elements that should not be considered elements of plural flow			The unit of performance is a group or team Tasks require interdependence, coordination and cooperation Tasks are conjunctive and require complementary participation[f] Rituals may be established to institutionalize social flow[g]		
Elements that are taking place outside of the control of the team				Team external factors Coaching style of the coach Support from supporters	

[a]Snow (2010)
[b]Sawyer (2007)
[c]Walker (2010)
[d]Mosek (2017)
[e]Csíkszentmihályi (1990)
[f]These are characteristics of the team, and thus part of the definition of a team, not team flow
[g]This is not an element but more an intervention to foster team flow

References

Csíkszentmihályi, M. (1990). *Flow: The psychology of optimal experience*. New York: Harper and Row.

Mosek, E. (2017). *Team flow: The missing piece in performance*. Doctoral dissertation. Victoria University.

Sawyer, R. K. (2007). *Group genius: The creative power of collaboration*. New York: Basic Books.

Snow, K. Y. (2010). *Work relationships that flow: Examining the interpersonal flow experience, knowledge sharing, and organizational commitment*. Doctoral dissertation. Claremont Graduate University. Retrieved from http://gradworks.umi.com/34/36/3436590.html.

Walker, C. J. (2010). Experiencing flow: Is doing it together better than doing it alone? *The Journal of Positive Psychology, 5*(1), 3–11.

The manufacturer's authorised representative in the EU is Springer Nature Customer Service Centre GmbH, Europaplatz 3, 69115 Heidelberg, Germany. If you have any concerns regarding our products, please contact ProductSafety@springernature.com

Printed and bound by CPI Group (UK) Ltd, Croydon, CR0 4YY
30/09/2026
02225664-0012